# Saved, Single and Pregnant

ROSALIND FRAZER

*Malikah,*

*May his power and love always lead you.*

*Love,*
*Rosalind*

ISBN 978-1-64079-024-7 (paperback)
ISBN 978-1-64079-025-4 (digital)

Copyright © 2017 by Rosalind Frazer
All rights reserved. No part of this publication may be reproduced, distributed, or transmitted in any form or by any means, including photocopying, recording, or other electronic or mechanical methods without the prior written permission of the publisher. For permission requests, solicit the publisher via the address below.

Christian Faith Publishing, Inc.
832 Park Avenue
Meadville, PA 16335
www.christianfaithpublishing.com

Printed in the United States of America

This page is dedicated to my "Mommy," so called by all seven of her children.

One thing I can say with a surety, my mother loved me.

I remember her telling me as a teenager, "If any man ever hit you, you come right back home to us, because We Love You."

Mommy, I miss you so much, not a day goes by that I don't think about you.

I'm so glad I know, you are safe in the Father's arms and I will see you again.

*The master said to him "Well done, my good and faithful servant." (Matt 25:23)*

This book is dedicated to the following people:

My son, Damani, you have been the joy of my life! I am so grateful for your love and understanding, especially when I shared the truth of my past. Your words I will never forget: "I understand and I am not mad at you." Your tender hug, I will cherish forever.

Janice C., thank you for being a true prayer partner and girlfriend. We have walked, cried, and prayed together as we shared our deepest, darkest secrets, shame, and bad decisions. Together we have found our Heavenly Father, and I am grateful.

Janine O., your teaching on sexual integrity was key in my liberation! I thank God for this powerful truth you tirelessly share. Never get weary in teaching; your voice and message are needed in the earth.

Pastor Je'nise, the prophetic in you is life changing! Without your prophetic word, encouragement, and inspiration, this book would not be here.

And to my Five Flowers: Peniel, Hope, Faith, Joy, and Israel. I love you all forever! I treated your lives as though they didn't matter, but giving dignity to your lives was instrumental in my healing. In accepting and acknowledging you all, my life has been healed and changed forever. Until we meet again. I love you all dearly!

# Contents

1. Preface .................................................. 7
2. Fears of Many Kinds ............................. 11
3. Before Salvation ................................... 14
4. Born Again ........................................... 19
5. The Call ................................................ 23
6. The Hospital ......................................... 25
7. The Desire ............................................ 27
8. Deceived .............................................. 29
9. A Seed in the Earth .............................. 32
10. Saved, Single and Pregnant ................. 38
11. The Decision ........................................ 41
12. Legalities ............................................. 44
13. Alone ................................................... 46
14. Transition ............................................ 48
15. Motherhood ........................................ 50
16. The Diagnosis ...................................... 53
17. The Second Diagnosis .......................... 56
18. The Third Diagnosis ............................. 59
19. His Working Grace ............................... 62

| | | |
|---|---|---|
| 20. | Decisions, Decisions | 65 |
| 21. | Turning of the Tides | 68 |
| 22. | A Gift | 71 |
| 23. | Angels | 73 |
| 24. | The Process | 80 |
| 25. | A Longing | 83 |
| 26. | Resilience | 88 |
| 27. | Lo-debar | 91 |
| 28. | Cargo | 96 |
| 29. | The Orphan Spirit | 101 |
| 30. | First Bind the Strongman | 106 |
| 31. | Love Is Like a Seed | 111 |
| 32. | At Last! | 115 |

# Preface

Sometimes life can become so painful, sorrowful, and difficult that believing God loves and cares about you is too hard to believe. At times, the pain is so intense you cannot even be sure He knows what is going on, much less believe His grace is sufficient. There are times when the voices of life's vicissitudes overwhelm you to the point where it becomes easy to believe the lie: God is not able, you really are defeated, and there is no need to keep going.

I've experienced some situations in life where it took everything within me to rise above the ashes. I have had different feelings such as, "This time, this situation has won," "I can't recover from this," "This time, I have lost it all," or "For sure, this is the situation that will take me out."

No matter what your thoughts, we all have had the same question at one time or another: is this problem too hard for God, or did this situation catch God by surprise?

I'm here to tell you, these are normal human thoughts and questions, so don't bother losing sleep condemning yourself because you had these feelings. Instead, rejoice in knowing that God cares,

His grace is sufficient, and He is and will always be in control, no matter the circumstance!

Yes, I have my share of stories about men and heartbreak, life's ups and downs, but the one that has given me the biggest challenge was when I conceived as a result of rape. That situation created such confusion, turmoil, rejection, and loneliness inside of me that it required everything in me to push myself to the next level and believe God cared and had worked it out for me to win.

How do you win when one person's selfish choice changes your life forever? You win knowing that one man's selfless act has changed your life forever. You win believing that "God knows the thoughts and plans he has concerning you, plans to prosper you and not to harm you, for good and not for evil, to give you a future and a hope" (Jer. 29:11).

As if that wasn't enough, six years later, I had the continuous sensation of pins and needles in my hands and feet for a full week. I was awake for an entire week, because the sensation would not ease up and at nights it became even more unnerving. Something was definitely wrong.

One thing I have learned about the voices of sickness: they are loudest in the midnight hours and wee hours of the mornings. I had to have this situation resolved, so I asked the doctor, "What is that, can you fix it?" Only to hear, "You have systemic lupus."

About a year later, I started experiencing incredible fatigue, shortness of breath, and incredibly low energy. Overall, I was just not feeling well, but I couldn't describe what was really wrong. Something was wrong, but neither myself nor my doctors at that time could identify it.

Then finally, a second riveting diagnosis. He said, "You have pulmonary hypertension, and it is progressing aggressively. On a scale of 1 to 10 of needing a lung transplant, you are about a 9, unless we get you on a pump, which you will have to be connected to twenty-four hours a day, 365 days a year for the rest of your life."

After living on an infusion pump for what supposedly was to be the rest of my life, God's mercy said, "No, this will only last 12.5

short years, for the testimony to others that you can live a normal life with two major chronic diseases."

The Logos word "You shall not die, but live to declare the works of the Lord" (Ps. 118:17) became *rhema* to me as I walked through the valley of the shadow of death. Looking back, I can clearly see that what the devil meant for evil, God turned for my good. Now I know these grueling life tests have provided a medium for God to show his power and for me to proclaim his name throughout all the earth (Ex. 9:16) so others may find hope in their valley experiences.

# Fears of Many Kinds

The dictionary defines *fear* as an unpleasant emotion caused by the belief that someone or something is dangerous, likely to cause pain, or a threat. Fear is a normal emotion designed to keep us safe. When fear is operating healthily in our lives, it alerts us to danger and triggers the fight-or-flight response.

In many cases, however, something unpleasant may have occurred in our lives and the aftermath of fearful thoughts bombard us, and before we know it, unhealthy fear, which brings torment, is activated and we no longer think on things that are true, honorable, right, pure, lovely, and admirable. Instead, we think about all of the dark what-ifs, causing the unhealthy fear to crop up, take residence within, torment us, and prevent us from moving forward in the purpose and destiny God has designed for each and every one of our lives.

In other words, as taught by Joyce Meyers, fear becomes "False Emotions Appearing Real." What happens in many of our lives as a result of our situations, instead of us casting down imaginations and shutting down fear based conversations within ourselves and through others, we entertain, meditate, and agree with them. Then we find ourselves crippled, immobilized, and unable to move forward in our lives because we are consumed with the what-if and then the inevitable "What coulda, woulda, shoulda" that we forfeited.

I say this from firsthand experience, because of fear of failure or rejection, criticism from others, of not getting it right, of looking stupid, or of what others will think, I have been slow to step out in new, unchartered waters in my life. You know, like writing this book, pursuing that third degree, applying for promotions, or even undertaking business ventures. It's like being in that ready stance, dancing back and forth before you actually jump into the rope when you are jumping double Dutch.

When we don't confront our fears, we will never know the end result of God's mind concerning our life's destiny, plan, and purpose. Confronting our fears many times can be a good thing, because we come to realize the thing that had so frightened us really has no power to harm us. Confrontation helps us take the power away from the person, situation, or thing.

Here are some quotes on the truth about dealing with fear:

Eleanor Roosevelt said: "You gain strength, courage and confidence by every experience in which you really stop to look fear in the face. You are able to say to yourself, ' I lived through this horror. I can take the next thing that comes along.' The danger lies in refusing to face the fear, in not daring to come to grips with it. If you fail anywhere along the line, it will take away your confidence. You must make yourself succeed every time. You must do the thing you think you cannot do."

President Franklin Delano Roosevelt said: "The only thing to fear is fear itself"

Victor Hugo said "Courage is not the absence of fear, but the mastery of it" and the late Susan Jeffers, Ph.D had the audacity to write a book entitled "Feel the Fear . . . .and Do It Anyway"

My strategy to deal with fear was to avoid, and here is where I would find false security. The problem with this tactic is you miss out on a lot, you talk yourself out of a lot, and you sit on the sidelines watching others pass you by, and in the end, you feel plain ole stuck.

Of course, we would all agree being raped, whether by a stranger or someone you know, is a legitimate horrible experience, and despite what doctors and the GOP Senate nominee Todd Akin may say, a woman can get pregnant from both instances, and it is devastating. So becoming a single parent because either you wanted to or you were thrust into it because of a failed relationship or the death of your partner is challenging enough; however, becoming a single parent without you even having a say in the matter to begin with magnifies fear of many kinds inside of you. Compounding that with two major chronic diseases, and your mind becomes overloaded with all kinds of scary thoughts about your future, your child's future, your health, your abilities, and your disabilities, and a plethora of negative thoughts can overwhelm you. Not to mention, thoughts of being sidelined and feelings of worthlessness, uselessness, rejection, etc.

In reality, because we live in a fallen world with broken people, we cannot escape situations that challenge our fortitude. Job said, "Man who is born of a woman is few of days and full of trouble" (Job 14:10). Remember, all our trials are merely tests—tests that challenge and test our elasticity, resiliency, and ability to stand and not faint during adversity. They push us to choose and trust God's sovereignty in our lives.

My intention is not to tell you whether your fears are real or unreal, justified or unjustified, but I am here to exhort you not to allow your fears to overtake and stop you from becoming an "overcomer" and to be all that God has created you to become.

# Before Salvation

I was born on the sunny isle of St. Thomas United States Virgin Islands. Virgin Islanders call St. Thomas the Rock or Rock City. We lived on the Rock until I was ten years old, then my family and I moved to Bronx, New York, which was affectionately known as the Boogie Down.

I enjoyed attending church and vacation Bible school when I was a little girl in Rock City. I loved learning all the songs, reciting the memory verses, and playing with my friends at church. Church was always a good experience for me.

We used to attend Calvary Baptist Church, which was pastored by the man called Brother Thomas. I don't remember him to be a very fiery preacher; in fact, I remember him as a very calm and mild-mannered man. I remember the older congregants would fall asleep after they sang and danced and he began to preach.

The church later branched off and moved from "in town to the country." We were having services at what I think now may have been a community room in the now-nonexistent Dunu Apartments. How I loved watching the adults have a good time playing instruments, singing, dancing, and testifying in church. I recall being embarrassed when my mother testified and even danced, as the other congregants did; however, I still enjoyed watching them all. Maybe this would explain why I unashamedly dance and worship in church today.

In 1976, a few months after my tenth birthday, we moved to the Big Apple, and I don't remember attending church anymore until I went away to college. I was a sophomore at Syracuse University when I visited a church in the community about once or twice. There was no commitment to going to church, nor was there even a semblance of knowledge that one could and should have a relationship with Jesus Christ.

After I graduated in 1987, I joined the military to help ease the pain of a broken heart. I remember meeting a soldier (we will call her Private Fox) who claimed to be a Rosicrucianist. At that time, I didn't know what a Rosicrucianist was, and I didn't know if she really was one, but I do know she was messing around with strange powders, drawing strange hexes on the floors, playing with Ouija boards, attempting to read the palms of soldiers, and only God knows what else she was doing with the willing and naive. I was like, "What in the world is this?" She was bent on presenting herself as having some mystical powers, but to me, she was only coming across as weird.

I distinctly remember one day she and a number of soldiers in our platoon were in a room and she was supposedly reading their palms. When I entered the room, they began coaxing me into having my palms read, something I was very hesitant to do. For some reason, I was one of the soldiers whose opinion others sought after and respected. I was very apprehensive, but they really wanted me to try.

I remember standing before her as she began asking personal questions, which I flat out refused to answer. I could see she was becoming frustrated. With a frustrated look and stern directive, she said, "You need to concentrate."

I told her, "I will not give you any answers. If you claim to have this power, let your god tell you about me. I will not have my God bow down to your god."

I remember the excitement around this activity ceased at that moment. Thank God for church up until age ten!

*"There shall not be found among you . . . anyone who practices divination or tells fortunes or interprets omens, or a sorcerer or a charmer or a medium or a necromancer or one who inquires of the dead, for whoever does these things is an abomination to the Lord." (Deut. 18:10-12)*

After returning from Basic Combat Training, Advanced Individual Training (AIT) and Officer Candidate School (OCS,) I continued on with life, seemingly without God. I believed in God, but I was clueless about going any further to get to know him. As far as I was concerned, I was a "good person," living as right as I knew.

Me and my sister Pat

When I was about twenty-two or twenty-three years old, my sister, Pat invited me and my then roommate Ingrid to visit a church she was attending in the Bronx. I only remember one thing that happened at the church: A man started speaking in his heavenly language in the midst of the congregation. A lady had just entered the service and stopped walking midstream as he spoke. She placed her bags beside her on the floor and immediately gave the interpretation. I must say I didn't really know about speaking in tongues and interpretation, but I knew that was a demonstration of the power of God. I never forgot that experience, because I believe that was the beginning stages of my spiritual awakening.

*"Pursue love, and earnestly desire the spiritual gifts, especially that you may prophesy. For one who speaks in a tongue speaks not to men but to God; for no one understands him, but he utters mysteries in the Spirit. On the other hand, the one who prophesies speaks to people for their up building and encouragement and consolation. The one who speaks in a tongue builds up himself, but the one who prophesies builds up the church. Now I want you all to speak in tongues, but even more to prophesy. The one who prophesies is greater than the one who speaks in tongues, unless someone interprets, so that the church may be built up." (1 Cor. 14:1–5)*

Ingrid and I, for the most part, were considered "nice girls." We were focused on our education and careers and what we thought were progressive ideas. We wanted a husband, kids, and anything else that demonstrated an orderly and successful life. We thought we were in control. We were not doing much in the way of partying and hanging out. Definitely we were not into drugs, alcohol, and I naively thought I was not promiscuous.

Me and my sister, Sue

I remember my other sister Sue and her boyfriend were visiting us one summer and she asked, "What do ya'll do? Ya'll might as well be Christians." That was the best advice anyone could have given us. Although my sister was being facetious, at the time, none of us realized she was speaking under the inspiration of the Holy Spirit.

In 1989 and 1990, Ingrid and I began visiting Temple Hills, Maryland, and the Fort Washington area, only to fall in love with it and eventually move away from New York City. My sister-in-law was attending Ebenezer AME Church at the time, where the pastors are Reverend Drs. Grainger and Joann Browning. She told us, "Come and see this African American church where the people are affluent and progressive. They drive luxury cars, live in nice big houses, and have a good time in church."

We visited the church and instantly agreed this was the life we were desiring. Without much reservation, we decided to pack our bags and say good-bye to the Big Apple forever. In 1990, we became members of Ebenezer AME Church.

# Born Again

In August 1991, I was in an adulterous relationship, which I knew was wrong, but I was willing to settle until something "better" came along. By now, we were regular church attendees at Sunday services and Wednesday-night Bible studies. I hadn't yet given my life to Christ, and I didn't know how far I was from God yet how close He was to me.

In August 1991, I attended one of the church's singles retreat. My reason for attending was to hopefully "land a husband." After all, it was a singles retreat. I had never attended a retreat before, so I had no idea what to expect. I really didn't know anyone and my roommate was unable to go, so I took the bold step to go and see what God had in store for me. Instead of landing a natural husband, I landed the best unintended husband anyone could ever hope for: the Lord of Hosts. God was faithful!

> *"For your Maker is your husband, the Lord of host is his name."* (Isa. 54:5)

I don't remember much of anything about the retreat, except the moment my life changed forever. I was sitting in service when the preacher Rev. Harold Hayes gave the call for salvation. I remember being too embarrassed to raise my hand and acknowledge I wasn't saved. After all, my thoughts were accusing and telling me, "Everyone will know you were perpetrating a fraud, attending the retreat and unsaved."

The Holy Spirit prompted the preacher with what I needed to hear, because the preacher immediately followed up with saying, "There may be someone here who is already saved, but all you want to do is make sure if Jesus came back tonight you would go with Him. Raise your hand."

It was like an out-of-body experience when I felt my hand rise up and I thought, *Hey, hand, what are you doing?*

The preacher then said, "Come forward and allow one of our ministers to pray with you."

Again, another out-of-body experience. I felt my body lift up out of the chair, and I started walking forward. Again, I thought to myself, *Hey, feet, where are you going?*

I went forward, and Minister Kelly Hayes prayed the prayer of salvation with me, changing my life forever. I was twenty-five years old.

> *"because if you confess with your mouth that Jesus is Lord and believe in your heart that God raised him from the dead, you will be saved." (Rom. 10:9)*

I went home and told my roommate, my sister-in-law, and everybody whom I came across what had happened at the retreat and how I had gotten saved. I wanted everyone to know what the Lord had done for me. I remember pointedly telling my roommate she wasn't saved because she hadn't prayed the prayer of salvation. This was very upsetting to her because she considered herself a devout Catholic. She followed up with her own research and soul searching. Shortly thereafter, she prayed the prayer of salvation to make sure she was saved.

Can you believe salvation is that simple? It comes only through belief in Christ and confession by the individual. Well, yes, it really is that simple. Although nothing more is required to receive salvation, proof of having the Holy Spirit should follow salvation by the person living a fruitful life, coupled with the evidence of a purged soul.

Can one continue in a lifestyle of bearing no fruit and profess to be a follower of Jesus Christ? I personally take issue with that position. What does this mean? It means after we say yes to the call, we get busy by allowing him to work through us and change us from the inside to the outside.

My roommate and I were both very excited about being saved, and God was just as excited about our answering his call. He made sure to keep the fire burning. We literally feasted on reading the Bible and could hardly put it down. God gave us three faithful disciples.

My roommate Ingrid

One was Tawanna, a coworker who faithfully met with us every Monday for one year uninterrupted. She read the Word with us, explained it, answered whatever questions we had, and prayed about whatever prayer needs or concerns we had. Then there was Sandra, another coworker from New York, and her friend April. They were excited when they learned about our salvation, and immediately came down from New York on a Friday evening bearing two Strong's Concordances and two Vine's Bible Dictionaries.

By the time they left our home that Sunday, we knew we wanted to have an intimate relationship with Jesus Christ. These three ladies, I must say, were the epitome of committed disciples of the Lord. Discipleship! These women were nonjudgmental and very patient with us. It was like sitting at the feet of Jesus. I believe their commitment to pouring into our lives may be one of the reasons we never returned to the world.

> *"Disciple- A follower and student of a mentor, teacher, or other figure. In Christianity the term disciple primarily refers to students of Jesus and is found in the New Testament only in the Gospels and Acts." (Wikipedia, the free encyclopedia)*

> *"Go therefore and make disciples of all the nations, baptizing them in the name of the Father and of the Son and of the Holy Spirit, teaching them to observe all things that I have commanded you." (Matt. 28:19)*

Now don't get me wrong, things weren't at all a bed of roses. There were, and still are, ups and downs, turns and bends, but the Word of God was true then and is true now. David said it best in Psalm 84:10: "A day in thy courts is better than a thousand, I would rather be a doorkeeper in the house of God than dwell in the tents of wickedness." At the risk of sounding too churchy, your worst day in God is better than your best day with the devil.

In case you were wondering what happened to the adulterous relationship, I brought that to an end. No more would I lower my standards and accept second best by being involved with someone else's husband. No more was I willing to consent to playing second fiddle. I would never do that again.

# The Call

When one becomes born again, there is excitement, anticipation, expectation, and the belief in the scripture in Philippians 4:13: "I can do all things through Christ who strengthens me." I believe it's in the infancy stages of our salvation wherein the Word of God is readily believed and applied without a lot of doubt. Babes in Christ are like daredevils: they believe "God said it and that settles it."

As the Word of God is read, the new believer is "crazy enough to believe it and courageous enough to do it." New believers earnestly trust God at his Word; after all, their eyes become open to the fact that all they had without Christ, as Paul said, should be counted for loss.

> "But what things were gain to me, these I have counted loss for Christ. Yet indeed I also count all things loss for the excellence of the knowledge of Christ Jesus my Lord, for whom I have suffered the loss of all things, and count them as rubbish, that I may gain Christ and be found in Him." (Phil. 3:7,8)

I literally couldn't get enough of the Word of God. It was exciting to me, and memorization came easy for me. More than anything, I wanted God to reveal my purpose. I wanted to know my place in the kingdom. What was I created to do?

I remember one day standing in front of the bathroom mirror, talking to myself (this is normal, right?). Suddenly, I heard a voice (not my own) say, "I have called you to be an evangelist."

I ran to get the dictionary to find the definition of *evangelist*. Then I hurried to get the Bible, and I saw the same message: "I have called you to be an evangelist."

Oh my goodness! I couldn't get to my roommate fast enough to show her the message, but I couldn't find it. I told her what I heard and saw. She said she believed me, but I felt as though she didn't; after all, I couldn't find the message I had so clearly seen and heard. However, I knew that was a message from God to me, and I believed it. I believed it then, and I still believe it today. As far as I was concerned, it was off to the races. Surely if God said it, shortly thereafter, I should be on the pulpit, right? Not.

# The Hospital

It was time for me to leave Ebenezer, where I had received salvation, and enter what I didn't know at the time was going to be my spiritual hospital. I was invited to attend the Church of the Great Commission (CGC). I was impressed with how the bishop and copastor brought the Word tag-team style that night and afterward sat on the steps in an informal way and "kicked it" with the young people. It felt like family, and I was even more amazed the bishop knew the names of all the people, considering the church size was medium to large. There was something about Bishop and Pastor that was touchable and caring to me.

Ebenezer's pastors were very nice also, but I never had the opportunity to directly work with them to know them outside of Sunday-worship service. Ebenezer was a very large church, and it was easy to get lost or hidden there, although I was involved in different ministries, I needed something a little more personal, where my pastors were more accessible to me.

After I met Bishop and Pastor, it was off to the races, and the teaching I was getting was food for my soul. I was now positioned in the right place for the right season. I didn't know the road to devastation, and difficulty was heading my way. I look back now and see by the mercies of God I was already where I needed to be: in the hospital, a deliverance ministry.

I was attending CGC when the relationship with my son's father started, and I am sad to say I never foresaw this whirlwind relationship ending the way it did. CGC is where I had to deal with the shame of being "saved, single, and pregnant." CGC is where I carried my child for nine months alone and was extremely embarrassed. After I delivered my son, there were numerous occasions of crying, shame, feelings of rejection, loneliness, bitterness, resentment, and deliverance experiences.

Here I was introduced to a significant part of my messy age. It was also where I learned to pray, read the Word, fast, and cling to God. It was in this spiritual hospital a prayer warrior was birthed.

# The Desire

The desire to marry a man of God and have a godly father for my children was ferociously alive in me. I wanted that husband more than anything else I could imagine. Having a godly husband would have surely complete me, I believed. In my mind, it was the final piece of the puzzle to a successful life.

Sometimes, you have such a burning desire for a thing that "it" actually has control of you. I really wanted to be a "true woman of God," but the desire for a husband was overtaking me. I had dated three good men, whom I would now admit were husband material. However, in my mind at the time, something very important was missing. I doubted their abilities to be able to cover me spiritually. I was saved, sanctified, and on fire for the Lord. I needed—or at least wanted—someone with the same level of fervor. After all, doesn't the Bible tell us not to be unequally yoked?

Do you know being unequally yoked can apply to two Christians also? In my naïveté, I didn't even think that could be possible. For sure there was no way I was going to be unequally yoked when I met my "Christian" Mr. Right.

Finally, I met Mr. Right, a saved man of God (hmmm). He was attractive, was the owner of a beautiful baritone singing voice, was dressed to kill, and boy, did he know the "Word." My prayers were finally answered, or so I thought.

> *"Beware of false prophets, who come to you in sheep's clothing but inwardly are ravenous wolves." (Matt 7:15)*

This man was ten years older than me, and yes, I will admit, I was smitten. The relationship was moving at a whirlwind speed. I saw every yellow and red light that signaled me to slow down, stop, take a second—even a third—look, but my desire or appetite was in control of me. We read the Word, discussed it, prayed, fasted together, and even sought the Lord about His will for our lives. I thought for sure I had found gold. No one could have told me this man wasn't sent by God.

Within the five months we had dated, I must say things were cropping up that were yelling, "Slow down, the light is yellow, don't run the red light, this may not be him!" All sorts of bells, whistles, sirens, and foghorns were sounding, but my appetite was in control of me. Caution was thrown to the wind.

It turned out my knight's shiny armor was really very tarnished. Had I really paid attention to all the yellow and red lights, I probably would not be writing a book on this particular topic. His beautiful lyrics were all lies. He wasn't really co-owning a house with his mother; instead, he was living in a bedroom in her house. He really wasn't working full time; it was part time. He really wasn't supportive of me; instead he was jealous of me. His words weren't really seasoned with grace, he was emotionally and verbally abusive, and, worst of all, he was not really divorced but separated. Unbeknownst to me, I was right back in another adulterous relationship, this time with a "saved man of God."

> *"What is desired in a man is steadfast love, and a poor man is better than a liar." (Prov. 19:22)*

# Deceived

I would say I should have applied brakes when I stepped on this roller coaster. Now, I must remind you what I encountered and the lessons I learned from this experience speaks to me, and if you find yourself in a similar relationship, I am not suggesting my end result will be yours. However, I will say if you see yellow and red lights, pay attention; don't just whiz by them, like I did. For sure, I bear some responsibility in this matter.

Let me start off by putting on the table we didn't have a relationship that was 100 percent celibate. We, like many Christian couples, found it difficult to obey the Word and God's instruction to flee from sexual immorality and make no provision for the flesh. Instead, we consented to disobedience. We never thought our disobedience would get out of hand and take us down the path we ended our relationship on.

The problem is, once we open the door to sin, we do not remain in the driver's seat to determine the cost and what the form of payment will be. Our consensual disobedience for sure gave the enemy a foothold for him to run rampant in our lives.

*"But if you do not do what is right, sin is crouching at your door, it desires to have you, but you must rule over it." (Gen 4:7)*

I remember when I first met him. I was twenty-seven years old and he was thirty-seven years old. He insisted he was divorced, not separated. I am sure if I knew he was separated we wouldn't have gone any further, because I had already made up in my mind that I didn't want to be in another adulterous relationship.

In all fairness to him, he held back the information, because he was unsure if the relationship would continue if I knew he was still married. His uncertainty was right; I would not have progressed in this relationship because I had already decided after I received Christ, I didn't want to be involved in someone else's marital situation again, not ever. Either way, it should have been my decision to make and not a decision I was deceived into.

Overall, there was a plethora of things he said and did that demonstrated he had no regard or respect for me as his sister in Christ or his "lady." To discuss or rehearse any of them at this time is unnecessary. However, now I understand the course of my life had changed forever. After a few more behaviors that chipped away at my self-esteem and self-worth, I decided to end the relationship. However, like too many women, by the time I decided to leave, I had allowed lies to take root. I knew I was unwilling to carry the baggage in the form of a relationship, but I was unaware I had decided to carry the effects of the negative relationship inside of me. The feeling of walking away was a relief, but the journey to be free from the effects of a bad decision would haunt me for many years to come.

Sometimes, or maybe a lot of times, when women find themselves tolerating poor behavior, I believe one of the reasons may be because their souls are hungry. Proverbs 27:7 says "The full soul loathes the honeycomb but to the hungry soul every bitter thing is sweet." Let us think upon the meaning of this verse in a simpler or natural context. At Thanksgiving time, a holiday that the table is filled with food, isn't there always food left over, because you are too full and satisfied? Even if your most favorite dish shows up to the table later, you just have to pass on it until you are hungry again. It's the same concept, when our souls are full with good things, love, joy, peace, security, healthy validation, we can say, no, to people and behaviors that are undesirable, because there is no yearning or longing for love and acceptance.

However, when people are hungry and lacking emotionally and spiritually, they will be slow at addressing or putting their foot down to cease negative behaviors or treatment, because there is a hunger or longing inside that needs to be satisfied, but unbeknownst to them, they settle for slop rather than feast on the Lord.

Subsequently, hungry women find themselves in certain life-threatening situations or emotionally devastating circumstances on the back end. Some things may appear minor and insignificant, but any misbehavior, lie, or mistreatment in the beginning, one should address up front. They may appear minor, but ask yourself, if the start of your relationship is being built on deception, lies, and abuse, is your relationship really healthy and worthy of you? What are you really building except monuments of nothingness?

> *"having a form of godliness but denying its power. Have nothing to do with such people . . . ( 2Tim 3:5-7)They are the kind who worm their way into homes and gain control over gullible women, who are loaded down with sins and are swayed by all kinds of evil desires, always learning but never able to come to a knowledge of truth." (2 Tim. 3:6–7)*

# A Seed in the Earth

About one month later, after I had ended my relationship with David (not his real name), I received a phone call from his wife. According to her, they were still married—not divorced, as he originally said. She said she had been encouraging him to tell me the truth as they were planning to reunite and as a young woman I should be able to move forward with my life.

I will spare the details of how my son was conceived, though it was not how I envisioned it would be. I never experienced the joys of announcing to my family and friends "we were expecting." I never had someone by my side to help satisfy my cravings and rub my aching feet. Although the entire pregnancy was healthy, the emotional challenge for me was overwhelming, but my son was and still is a joy to this day.

God's word really is true, it rains on the just and the unjust and the sun shines on them both. So a helpful way of looking at our life situations are to remember, no matter what we go through he still promises that "all things work together for the good of those who love him, who have been called according to his purpose." What is his purpose you may be asking yourself, Ro 8:29 says it is so we may be conformed to his image. So I dare say, no matter how much we delight ourselves in him we will never escape trials, struggles, and tribulations in this life. Our life experiences are not in vain. No matter what we go through, God has a way of using it for his glory. It all depends on our willingness to trust him with the difficult and dark moments that shouts nothing other than hopelessness, despair, and death in the beginning. I believe like Joseph in Gen 50:20 the enemy may have thought it for evil against you, but God always means it for our good!

I say, don't focus on the trial or the circumstances used. In Nahum 1:12 God said "Though they are at full strength and many, they will be cut down and pass away." Yes, our enemies and situations seem to come against us at full throttle, but God is saying, they will be cut down and we will no longer be plagued by them, they will be no more. So I say, instead of focusing on our trials and circumstances, focus on the work He is doing, the purifying process to bring you forth as pure gold. Whatever test you are going through, whatever circumstance, or situation is used, know beauty can arise from ashes. It doesn't have to destroy you; it will *not* destroy you, nothing you are going through is meant to destroy you. It is all useful and purpose driven, so whatever the devil meant for evil, God will turn it for your good. So let's praise Him and repent where repentance is needed and praise him that we already have the victory. It took me years to grasp this understanding. It wasn't until speaking with Pastor Jenise was I able to see, God is most concerned about the product and not as overly concerned about the process. We in our finite minds are more concerned about the process, because our process at times can be so painful, long and seemingly hopeless.

We are God's instruments. We must be open to being played however He chooses. In Isaiah 45 God took a pagan, King Cyrus, and used him as an instrument in his hand for his purpose, which was to deliver Israel from their captivity.

God went on to say in vs 9 "Woe to him who strives with him who formed him." Here it is clear that it is God's prerogative to use us how he desires and in what way he desires and it is probably not the wisest thing to argue with him about how he chooses to use you.

In vs 11 he said "Ask me of things to come; will you command me concerning my children and the work of my hands?"

In other words, God is the potter and we are the clay, the purpose and plan belong to him and he works it how he sees fit. Now this will create some level of controversy when we think on the sovereignty of God and free will, but for the purposes of this point, we will stick to vs 1 where the Lord acknowledges Cyrus was an instrument in his hand, "Whose right hand I have grasped to subdue nations before him." It is clear in this verse God is saying without a doubt, he used King Cyrus in the way he wanted to, to bring about God's desired outcome. So in my level of understanding, I will say, we are instruments in his hands.

I would also like to think we are not only instruments in the hands of the Lord, but we are also deadly weapons in his hands to the kingdom of darkness. There seems to be theological uncertainty as to who Jeremiah 51:20 ("You are my hammer or weapon of war") was addressing, was it Cyrus, the army of the Medes and Persians, or Babylon?

If I could use my prophetic license I would like to take some liberty and suggest that since the bible is replete with scriptures that demonstrated how the children of Israel had to physically fight; Today New Testament believers understand we do not wrestle against flesh and blood. We have weapons of warfare that are not carnal but mighty though God for a spiritual battle we cannot opt out of; and God our Commander – in Chief is described as a "Man of War." He has given us an entire armour (Eph 6:10-18) to put on and eight weapons to fight with: praise, the word of God, the blood of Jesus, prayer, your testimony, the expressed gifts of the Holy Spirit, the name of Jesus and fasting (http: // www.Christian - faith.com/ forjesus/weapons- of- spiritual-warfare) and he does what he pleases (Ps 115:3) I would say, it is safe to say, we are weapons in his hands.

Acknowledging that we are instruments and weapons in his hands may be hard to grasp for some, but for others we understand when Paul says in 1 Co 1:27 "But God chose what the world considers nonsense to put wise people to shame. God chose what the world considers weak to put what is strong to shame." When we reflect on life's difficulties and hear the many stories of triumph it really does make sense when Paul said in 1 Co 1:18 "For the message of the cross is foolishness to those who are perishing but to us who are being saved it is the power of God."

Every strum of us as instruments is a strum of redemption for someone. To some we bring deliverance, to others we bring healing, to some hope, others freedom, some victory, some mending and restoration for others. However God chooses to play us, we should be available and willing, because he will never play us in a wrong key. Be open, be ready to make sweet melody in his hands, and accept the note or chord that he strums you in; it will be melodious, whether soft or loud, hard or easy. Don't become offended as he makes sweet music with you. I have seen some dark situations occur in not only my life, but others as well and it looks like, no way can this work for good . . . But God! When you hear the stories of redemption, you have no choice but to admit there is a God.

This is why it is important for us to find the courage to tell our stories. Testifying about your dark times takes tremendous courage, but o' the joy when someone else decides they can live and do better because you chose to humble yourself and reveal your weakness and triumph.

> *"And they overcame by the blood of the lamb and the word of their testimony; and they loved not their lives unto death."*
> *(Rev 12:11)*

No matter the situation, whether you are wrong or right, the good news is God still cares for you! He never stops caring, and he is patiently waiting for you to get up and get right back on the horse. Don't wallow in your losses, failures, and disappointments; they serve a purpose. They show you, you, and they add character, shape, and life to your story. Someone is waiting to hear how you fell and then got up. Get up regardless, because he cares for you!

How do you see yourself? If you are ordinary, will you fight to stay ordinary, or will you fight to be extraordinary?

My college girlfriends saw me at one of the darkest moments in my life, after they watched the stranger get on the elevator. They couldn't understand: was I crying tears of joy because we hadn't seen each other in years, or did the stranger at the elevator have something to do with my tears?

They finally thought to ask the question "Did the man who just got on the elevator have anything to do with your tears?" My answer was, "Yes." I was hysterical! I had just been violated.

The next question was, "Do you want to call the police?"

Fearing the exposure of my past and knowing how the victim is somehow always to blame, I chose not to involve the police. I decided to try and forget the entire thing and suppress the reality the best way I knew how.

After many nights of tears, I had to make a decision: was I going to be a victim or a survivor? The decision was made: I was going to be a survivor and live for God. As far as I was concerned, I didn't have pleasant thoughts about him, but with determination and a change of perspective, an unpleasant situation brought a young man I wouldn't trade for the world. "A seed was now in the earth."

A Seed is in the Earth

After going through a traumatic experience, I had to decide how I was going to cope, what type of coping strategy I was going to employ, and, most of all, if I was going to still be victorious.

# Saved, Single and Pregnant

I was twenty-seven years old when the early pregnancy test (EPT) read positive. That should have been joyous news, but due to the circumstances, I must admit it was everything but joyous. The EPT didn't lie. It was the beginning of a journey that felt like defeat. I was "saved, single, and pregnant."

It was at a family party where I told my siblings the shocking news. I remember the air left the room when I disclosed the news and how upset my brothers were. They were especially upset because they wanted to protect their youngest sister; a woman in their family had been violated. Wisdom told me not to give any information about the man who had changed my life forever. As far as I was concerned, he had done enough damage. I was not going to set my brothers up to put themselves in a situation that would add sorrow to sorrow. They too had families, children, and wives who needed them.

To this day, I applaud my brothers for the incredible strength and restraint it took to honor my wishes not to fight. I reminded them of Romans 12:19: "Vengeance is mine, I will repay says the Lord." Prophet L. Donnell Goss said, "It took more strength for Jesus to stay on the cross than for him to come down." I would say the same for my brothers; it took tremendous strength for them not to confront this man to defend my honor.

Saved Single and Pregnant
Me - December, 1993

The nine months I carried my son was a very lonely time for me. The entire dream of sharing this "wonderful time" with someone special was now only a figment of my imagination. My dream of being blissfully happy, eating pickles and ice cream, with swollen feet and my beloved husband next to me was now forever a fantasy too painful to even think about.

I remember going about my pregnancy thinking how different I wished my pregnancy experience could have been. I didn't have a wedding band on my finger, a constant reminder to me that sin had entered in and had seemingly won. Now "I" carried the heavy burden of loneliness, pain, rejection, and embarrassment.

Attending church was even lonelier. I remember one Sunday the pain overwhelmed me to the point of causing me to scream uncontrollably during the service. Many of the women surrounded me with intentions to help, but when I told them the source of my pain, it seemed like all they could offer were their condolences. It appeared like this news was far too great a situation for even God to handle. I read their faces and realized this circumstance was greater than I could even imagine.

The associate pastor's wife was the only person who was able to articulate that God was still in control, and with all authority, she prophesied with the greatest conviction, saying, "You are not carrying Ishmael! You are not carrying Ishmael!"

I knew that was the Lord speaking to me, because I had recently read the text about Abraham, Sarah, and Hagar, and I had decided I was carrying Ishmael.

Condemnation hovered over me daily, so I had to trust Him that he had forgiven me and He was with me in the midst of my storm.

I was embarrassed for the entire nine months of my pregnancy—embarrassed at work, at church, around my family, at the doctor's office. Anywhere outside of being alone, I was embarrassed. I was ashamed that I was saved, single, and pregnant. I was ashamed that I wasn't married, so I pondered the thought of wearing a wedding band to deceive the people and make them think I was married. Only God knew the real pain and loneliness I was carrying inside of me. That pain and loneliness was more difficult to carry than my baby.

What tore at me more than anything was I was such a bold witness for the Lord. I used to unashamedly tell the world about my Savior. Now I felt like I had to sit down, be seen but not be heard. How could this happen to me? I thought I was on my way to becoming a powerful evangelist for the Lord.

# The Decision

When I told my baby's father the outcome of his poor choice and selfish decision, he immediately took the familiar road: "Have an abortion," he callously said.

I told him that was not an option and I didn't believe it was in line with God's plan for my life.

He said, "Everybody else does it."

It earnestly wasn't an option for me, because I had done it before, and something inside of me kept warning me if I did it again either I would either not get up from the table or when I did want to have a child I wouldn't be able to. Now my stance of being pro-life was being put to the test. It was easy to be pro-choice all through high school and college when God was nowhere in my thoughts and I was the captain of my own ship. However, being pro-life because I had Christian convictions was a completely different matter. God was on my mind and in my heart. Pleasing Him was important to me.

I was a staunch pro-choicer before salvation, I had it all figured out. It was my body, my choice. I knew what was best for me and no one would decide otherwise. I knew the Isley Brothers were singing to me when they sang "Its your thing, do what you wanna do. The next time I became pregnant, I would be in a loving marital relationship. I would have a loving, caring husband, and there would be no need to have to have to make a decision about keeping or terminating a pregnancy.

When I became a Christian, I was happy to say I was no longer pro-choice. I was now, unbeknownst to me, hypocritically pro-life. I say this with a humbled heart, because my change of heart was predicated on the fact that I had made my decisions and I thought I had gotten away scot-free. I could now go about my merry way and never be faced with having to choose between keeping or terminating an unplanned pregnancy again.

I have since learned taking a stand on either side of the fence is very difficult, and I understand the passion both sides take about this very sensitive issue. However, I would be remiss if I did not share, the scriptures are unequivocally clear "before we were formed in our mother's womb, God knew us and set us apart" (Jer. 1:5) and Psalm 127:3 tells us "Children are a gift from the Lord; they are a reward from him."

According to Bill and Sue Banks, in the book "Ministering to Abortion's Aftermath" they say "Abortion has been offered as a panacea for women. Rather than solving problems for women it has been shown to cause deep seated guilt and often mental illness." It is important for one to know the whole truth before they make an abortion decision and the truth is there will be the consequences of the aftermath to pay. In addition, I must say, when we are abortion minded with children already in the womb, we invite the spirit of rejection into our unborn child and a host of other demonic activities that manifests in our children's personalities and our relationship with them. Moreover, when one follows through and has an abortion(s) there are a myriad of problems the parents may deal with individually or as a couple, whether or not they realize the abortion's aftermath is the root cause. My decision not to abort my son is a decision I don't regret, and I am super elated I made the decision to keep him. However, I can't deny the many problems we have encountered realistically, because he sensed rejection from the womb. I do not condemn or judge those whose decision is different from mine. I will say, I do not believe aborting a child is in line with God's perfect and best plan for us and I do not believe the decision to abort will be without consequence. I can assure you, taking a stand for life wasn't easy, nor did it lack turmoil inside of me when I was in a difficult predicament, but the fruit of my decision has brought tremendous joy to my heart as I experience God's grace and power in our lives daily.

I believe my son's father, David, was also faced with a difficult decision because to his credit, he is a wonderful father to his other children. His seemingly ill-informed easy solution was an attempt to cover his mistake and erase from his memory what he had done, so adding insult to the injury, he asked, "Are you sure I am the father?"

# Legalities

I decided I would not take this matter to court. We were believers, and I believed the Word of God could guide me through this storm. Paul said in 1 Corinthians 6:1,

> "Dare any of you, having a matter against another, go to law before the unrighteous, and not before the saints? Do you not know that the saints will judge the world? And if the world will be judged by you, are you unworthy to judge the smallest matters?"

Instead, I told my bishop and my pastor about the situation. One of my best girlfriends, who is a Christian and an attorney, had agreed to represent me. My bishop contacted David's pastor, and we set up a meeting. We were going to handle this matter biblically and enlist his support to be responsible for the life that now was created.

A meeting was set at the church, but lo and behold, David was a no-show. His pastor was at a loss; he said he had made contact with David and David had agreed to attend the meeting. The only thing the clergies could do at that point was pray for me and tell me it was up to me if I wanted to get the law involved; after all, his actions up to this point questioned whether or not he was truly a believer.

I reached out to David again, and he gave some lame excuse as to why he didn't show for the meeting.

# Alone

I believe children need both parents, and if the parents can't be together, they should at least be able to coparent. I tried to have amicable interactions with him, but that only lasted until I was in my fifth month of pregnancy, because the stress he brought to the conversations was greater than I was able to handle.

Somewhere into my fifth month of pregnancy, I believe the Lord impressed in my spirit, "The devil is trying to kill your baby, and he is using the baby's father to do it." Immediately, I cut off all interactions with David, changed addresses, and had no further contact with him until my son was five years old when he contacted us.

Being saved, single, and pregnant plagued me throughout my pregnancy, and to be truthful, it has etched a place in my heart that I will take to my grave.

I was lonely and felt like giving up, but I made a decision I would trust God in the midst of adversity. I was not alone because God was with me. It took everything inside of me to hold my head up and not give in. So I quoted the scriptures, "When I fall, I will arise." I encouraged myself daily by reminding myself trouble doesn't last always: "Weeping may endure for a night, but joy comes in the morning." One day, "I shall arise."

I remember sharing with my pastor that I was not feeling connected to the baby inside me. She was compassionate and understanding about my honesty. She said, "Anoint your belly every day from now until the baby is born. Pray for your baby, and I guarantee you will love that baby when he/she is born."

I did as she instructed, and would you know when I saw his beautiful little face all the feelings of indifference were no more. Now, I was a lioness with a cub to protect.

In 2 Kings 5:1–14, the prophet Elisha told Naaman to go dip in the Jordan seven times and he would be healed of his leprosy. Naaman, being the commander to the Syrian Army, was offended because he thought he deserved to be greeted and given special instructions in perhaps a more spiritual or what he would have considered a more dignified or respectable way. Then with high-mindedness, he even thought the prophet could have at least sent him to cleaner waters than the Jordan.

Eventually, the servants were able to convince him that he should obey the prophet and do as instructed. Naaman acquiesced, and to his surprise, he was healed of leprosy, and his flesh was restored like the flesh of a little child, and he was clean.

I point you to this chapter of the Bible to show you the power of the prophetic. When God speaks through his prophets and gives us instruction so we can receive healing, restoration, and deliverance, we need to heed the voice of the prophet and do exactly what we are instructed to do. Our trust helps us to stand, and we demonstrate our faith by our obedience.

> *"Believe in the Lord your God, and you will be able to stand firm. Believe in his prophets, and you will succeed."* (2 Chron. 20:20)

# Transition

I didn't know what the effect of being saved, single, and pregnant would have on my life. I only knew my life would never be the same again; only God knew what was in store for me. I knew that having a child had already sidelined me from some relationships with potential mates. There are some men who simply do not want a "ready-made" family, and I was not willing to leave my son at home while I went out to pursue a man. I would just wait and let God bring the right man to us.

My little bundle of joy was definitely worth the sacrifice. Single parenting was a press, challenge, fight, struggle, push—whatever you want to call it. It was not easy. Fighting to stay in the game of life took more work than I could have imagined.

Three years later, my pastor passed away. She was only forty-five years old. Her passing was devastating to the church, and it prompted me to move on to the next level in my spiritual life. Shortly after her death, I was impressed by the Holy Spirit it was time to transition from the hospital and move to the next level in my Christian sojourn. It was a hard decision to make, because here was where I connected to very strong seasoned prayer warriors—solid, mature women of God. Here was where I met my "spiritual mother." At this ministry, I received some healing and deliverance.

> *"Older women likewise are to be reverent in behavior, not slanderers or slaves to much wine. They are to teach what is good, and so train the young women to love their husbands and children, to be self-controlled, pure, working at home, kind and submissive to their own husbands, that the word of God may not be reviled." (Titus 2:3–4)*

The question was, where were we going? I prayed and asked God for direction. He led me to 1 Kings 17:8–16 (about Elijah and the widow). One day, I decided out of the blue (or what I thought was out of the blue) to visit the church my previous roommate attended. I didn't mind shouting on occasion with those Pentecostals at that little church. I visited this small Pentecostal Church where they would unashamedly dance for hours and testify.

The night I visited, there was a guest pastor at the church, and I could tell you if I am lying, I am flying. That pastor spoke on everything I had been talking to God about; the revelation he brought and the way he expounded on the Word seemed to quench the thirst and satisfy the hunger my soul was experiencing for so long.

For the first time in a long time, my thirsty and hungry soul was being satisfied. The prophetic Word was clear that night. The pastor of the small Pentecostal Church I had visited was a widow, and like Elijah and the widow, God provided the food I needed by way of the visiting pastor, served by the hands of the widow.

My son was only three years old at the time when we started visiting this small family-oriented church. After a few visits, I decided this was where God was leading us, so I submitted my letter of resignation to CGC. The two of us were transitioning to a new church family that were also very invested in the lives of their children.

# Motherhood

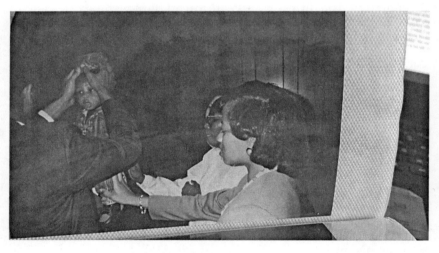

Dedication Day

"So now I have also dedicated him to the Lord; as long as he lives he is dedicated to the Lord" 1 Sam 1:28

I loved my son, and I wanted more than anything to raise a man of God. I wanted him to be the best man God created him to be. I wanted him to be well adjusted, to have the best opportunities, a good education, and a great shot at life as he became a productive citizen. What parent doesn't desire the best for their child(ren)? I was determined neither he nor I would be a statistic. Without a father figure present, I would trust the Lord at all cost to make sure I took good care of him. I was not going to take out my anger and resentment of his father's choices on him. I was determined I wouldn't give up on God. Being a saved single mom was not easy then, and it is still not easy now, twenty-three years later. I give a colossal-size kudos to the single parents who chose to hang in there! No condemnation to the parents who chose otherwise.

I wish I could say I did it all right, but I didn't. Yes, I dated a few times, because more than anything I wanted companionship and a "daddy" for my son. I felt the pain he was feeling of not having a father in his life. However, I felt the rejection of never having a committed man come alongside us and say, "Here I am, I will accept the opportunity to love you and 'our' son."

Motherhood-- I love my boy!

The loneliness turned into feelings of rejection. Rejection turned into anger and some capriciousness along the way. No need to recount them all in this story; we will have numerous opportunities to discuss them in person.

I stayed very connected to the church and was in a committed relationship with Jesus Christ. I was very active in my son's life. We attended church regularly. He attended good schools, was active in sports, took music lessons, traveled, and had the support of family and friends. We resided in safe neighborhoods. I say this not to brag, boast, or look down on those who are or were less fortunate but to plug the importance of education and knowing the Lord Jesus Christ. I believe having a college education, gave me an edge to successfully compete in the job market. Though a curve ball was thrown my way, I had the means, discipline, and wherewithal to fight.

I believe education is important, and too many young people are doing themselves a disservice by casting education aside for immediate, short-lived gratification. I also believe that knowing Christ saved me from some devastation that bad decisions or life brings our way.

Moreover, the crux and honest truth of the matter is although I appeared to be holding it together and seemingly still moving forward, the real truth is I was drowning. I was drowning in feelings of rejection, despair, loneliness, guilt, and anger. I wanted so much for us to be wanted. I wanted someone to sincerely care for us, fight for us, and be concerned about what was going on with us. Again, I was greatly consumed by my desires, and the thought of being a powerful voice for God was being silenced by life.

# The Diagnosis

At thirty-three years old, I was connected to a church that really felt supportive and like a real family. It was not the romantic relationship I desired, but the people were definitely supportive of my son and me. I felt as though we were heading upward. I was active in church, and felt like I was in a good place emotionally. Being in a good place doesn't mean everything is all fixed, but it does mean you have peace with God and you are able to stand under the pressures. In this place there are still hills and valleys, twists and turns, lows and highs, but at least your mind is focused and you know God is with you.

Have you ever experienced being on this course and all of a sudden another storm comes and knocks the wind right out of your sail?

Well, it happened to me right when I felt like I was getting my mojo back. One day, I had the continuous sensation of pins and needles in my hands and feet, and this sensation continued nonstop for a week straight. I was awake for one full week, because the sensation would not ease up, and at nights, it became even more intense. Something was definitely wrong. One thing I have learned about the voices of sickness: they are loudest in the midnight hours and the wee hours of the mornings. I had to have this situation resolved, so I went to the doctor, only to learn I had systemic lupus erythematosus (SLE).

Lupus. What was that? It sounded as though it was going to instantly kill me. I had never heard about lupus; all I knew from the doctor was it was an autoimmune disease. With autoimmune diseases, your body is deceived by itself and begins to attack itself, thinking there is an invasion of something foreign that it must fight. This would be good if there really was a foreigner to attack, but the body is perceiving itself as a foreigner, and it fights against itself.

In addition, auto immune diseases can affect virtually any organ of the body. It attacks healthy tissues, causing a swelling known as inflammation. Inflammation can occur in the skin, muscles, or joints (information taken from the Arthritis Society). In this attack on self, many different major organs such as the brain, skin, kidneys, lungs, heart, and blood can become affected. When any of the major organs are attacked, one is diagnosed with systemic lupus. The attack of the skin or joints is known as discoid lupus. There is no known cause for this disorder.

Due to the fact this disease does not possess a single track, the initial diagnosis is difficult. Patients are affected in different ways; therefore, physicians and medical professionals find themselves engaged in a battle of chasing symptoms that appear briefly and disappear. The occurrence of a more serious disease could halt the investigation and identification of the primary culprit, lupus.

For example, a patient could be diagnosed as having pulmonary hypertension, and the treatment would start and end there when, in fact, lupus is the root nemesis. The lupus goes untreated, and would remain in its very active and aggressive state, able to wreak more havoc on the body.

I remember making up in my mind that I would not give in to this diagnosis. I would pray, research, and try alternative remedies. I didn't want the contemporary medications of the Plaquenil and Prednisone the doctor discussed with me. I felt like that would speak against my faith and trust in God.

However, as time was passing and the alternative remedies were not. I spoke with my pastors about taking conventional medication and what that would mean about my faith in God's ability to heal. After speaking with them, I readily accepted God had given the doctors wisdom to diagnose and treat illnesses. I decided to put my faith and trust in God as I followed what the doctors were advising me to do. Thank God I combined my faith with works because I am here to reiterate what James said that was great wisdom: "Faith without works is dead."

> "What does it profit, my brethren, if someone says he has faith but does not have works? Can faith save him? "But someone will say, "You have faith, and I have works." Show me your faith without your works, and I will show you my faith by my works." You believe that there is one God. You do well. Even the demons believe- and tremble! But do you want to know, O foolish man, that faith without works is dead?" (James 2:14,18)

After I started taking the conventional medication, things were seemingly back to normal. Little did I know a more vicious disease was brewing underneath it all. Remember, lupus, when it is active, can wreak havoc in other organs of the body. In systemic lupus—which, of course, I would get stuck with—my pulmonary artery was under serious attack.

# The Second Diagnosis

As far as I was concerned, I had gone through a lot in eight years. I had been on enough floors screaming, rolling in agony, with church people trying to get me "delivered and set free" from whatever was tormenting and causing me significant heart pain. I appeared to have it together on the outside, but at home, it was difficult for me not to yell and be angry.

My son was hyperactive, and no matter how involved I was in his life, school, and social activities, teachers and administrators were calling me regularly to complain about something he had done. I couldn't understand why he was "behaving" this way. I would ask myself, why is he adding to my sorrow? Whenever the teachers attempted to suggest to me he could possibly be ADHD and should be tested, I adamantly rejected it. Not my child, not this "black male." They were not going to label and medicate him; he was not going to be another statistic. As far as I was concerned, God had created him to be great and proclaim His name in the earth, and I was not going to allow anyone to tell me otherwise.

He was in the fourth grade when his teacher, an African American lady, pulled me aside and said, "You need to have your son tested, I believe he has ADHD."

I immediately went into my spiel of the "white man" always trying to diagnose and medicate young "black men." She allowed me to speak, then she looked me square in the eyes and said, "I hear what you are saying, but this one needs to be tested." She went on to tell me not testing him and getting him the proper treatment and service would be a grave disservice to him.

I really felt like my world was crumbling. I was a saved, strong, educated woman. A social worker, to top things off. How could life be handing me continuous lemons? Wasn't I supposed to have things working in my favor? After all, wasn't coming to Jesus supposed to make my life all better? How could everything be working against me? Wasn't I supposed to have it all together?

For real, I thought knowing God meant you could just quote the Word and life would automatically line up. Instead, here I was being dealt one bad hand after another.

I had my son tested, and much to my chagrin, he was diagnosed as having ADHD.

Snider, Busch, and Arrowood (2003) cites the National Institute of Health Consensus statement, 1998, as saying attention deficit hyperactivity disorder (ADHD) is the most commonly diagnosed psychiatric disorder of childhood.

The DSM-5 cites ADHD as a pattern of behavior present in multiple settings (e.g., school and home) that can result in performance issues in social, educational, or work settings. As in DSM-IV, symptoms will be divided into two categories of inattention and hyperactivity and impulsivity that include behaviors like failing to pay close attention to details, difficulty organizing tasks and activities, excessive talking, fidgeting, or having an inability to remain seated in appropriate situations.

Children must have at least six symptoms from either (or both) the inattention group of criteria and the hyperactivity and impulsivity criteria while older adolescents and adults (over age seventeen) must present with five.

The attention aspect of the disorder must have nine characteristic features, with six of the symptoms needing to be manifested persistently for six months. The hyperactivity-impulsivity aspect also has nine characteristic features, and six of the nine must also be persistently present for six months.

In the DSM-5, the criteria suggests that some of the impairment should have been present before age twelve, compared to the DSM-IV that stated the age of onset as age seven and should be present in two or more settings (i.e., school and at home).

To be honest, I was embarrassed. I was embarrassed because I wanted my life and my child to be perfect so we could show the world that we could do this thing just fine without a father; with God on our side, He was more than the world against us. In other words, I wanted to prove the doubters wrong and shut the mouths of the naysayers.

In reality, his diagnosis felt like another blow with a hammer. I tried to pray away his hyperactivity, yell it away, discipline it away, ignore it away, medicate it away, counsel and tutor it away, and even excuse it away. I tried everything I could think of to support my child, but it seemed to be getting the best of him and me. The trials and tests of life appeared to be defeating me.

> *"Consider it pure joy, my brothers and sisters, whenever you face trials of many kinds because you know that the testing of your faith produces perseverance. Let perseverance finish its work so that you may be mature and complete, not lacking anything." (James 1:2-4)*

# The Third Diagnosis

About a year later, I started experiencing unidentifiable, peculiar, bothersome-yet-hard-to-describe medical issues that stumped several doctors. Most affected was my breathing. I noticed that walking was instantly becoming laborious for me. I couldn't walk fast even if I had to be somewhere in a hurry. I remember running late for a 9:00 a.m. court hearing. I felt like I was literally sauntering into the courthouse. That was striking to me, because being from New York, I always walked in a hurried pace, and I knew court was not the place to show up late.

After the hearing, my coworker and I had to walk up the garage stairs, and when I entered my car, I practically passed out. My coworker frantically helped unbutton my shirt, fanned, and gave me water and her snack bar. I chalked it all up to not eating breakfast. I think it was scarier for her than it was for me.

A few days later, I was carrying some grocery bags up to my second-floor apartment, and my eight-year-old son was sitting on the living room floor watching television. When I brought in the last bag, I lay on the floor, completely out of breath. I remember him asking, "Mommy, do you want me to call 911?"

I said, "No, I'm fine."

It was two hours later when I came to myself lying in the same place where I had laid down when I entered the apartment. I remember the entire event took two hours, because I looked at the clock before I passed out.

I immediately made a doctor's appointment after that second episode. I was a single working mom, and I couldn't afford to miss being around to care for my son or be off work for any extended period of time.

I went to the doctor and explained what had happened on those two occasions. I was a very good historian, and I still am today. I thought with me giving him very specific details he would have no problem diagnosing the problem, fixing it, and sending me on my way.

Instead, it took weeks of him being puzzled and sending me on for further testing. The ultrasound test returned, and all he knew was the ultrasound had shown I had something large in my chest. He didn't know what it was, so he couldn't release me to return to work. The amazing thing to me was, the doctors were really not following up with each other as they sent me from this doctor to that doctor for yet another test.

All I know was I was feeling very exhausted twenty-four hours a day. I felt like if I just got one good sleep in, I would be rejuvenated. I didn't even have the energy to voice my objections with the handling of my care, because I was really too tired. Wherever I went, I walked slowly, and I would actually fall asleep sitting or standing, it didn't matter. I was just tired.

Finally, the doctor sent me to Inova Alexandria Hospital to get an echocardiogram. Would you believe I fell asleep in the waiting room and when I awakened all the other patients waiting were seen and gone, including the office staff and the radiologist? The lights were off, the doors were locked, and everyone had gone home. I was disoriented and confused because it didn't seem like I was asleep for very long. I went to the security guard and complained. I don't know how this happened, but he called around to several people, and a radiologist was sent back to that office specifically to see me.

> *"In my distress I called upon the Lord, And cried out to my God, He heard my voice from His temple, And my cry came before Him, even to His ears... He delivered me from my strong enemy... The Lord was my support." (Ps. 18:4–6, 17–18)*

The radiologist who came back to assist me after hours took his time with me, and he reluctantly told me what he had found. However, before telling me, he made me promise not to tell the doctor he had told me. I promised, and he told me, "You have pulmonary hypertension, and it is very serious."

I had never heard of that before, so I naively asked, "Can you fix it while I'm here? I really need to get back to work."

He was honest with me. "It is going to be a while before you return to work."

My rheumatologist was the one who officially delivered the third riveting diagnosis: "You have pulmonary hypertension."

What is that, I asked.

All he could really tell me was it was rare and very serious. He really wasn't giving much beyond that. I asked about treatment, and he delivered the hammer. He said there wasn't much that is known about it.

First, he said, "I will try you on calcium channel blockers, and if that doesn't work, then I will try you on beta-blockers, and if that doesn't work, then you will need a heart and lung transplant."

"What?" I stared at him as though he had grown three heads. The thing that really threw me off was how flippant he was as he said it.

My head was reeling as I left his office. I went outside and called for my ride, and she told me she couldn't return for me. I was stranded, standing all alone in the parking lot after hearing devastating news. I didn't know what else to do, so I called my pastor and bawled uncontrollably in the parking lot, outside the doctor's office. God had mercy on me, and once again, he heard my cry, and my ride pulled up and took me home.

# His Working Grace

From that point on, my girl Toya began the long haul with me. She made numerous doctor's appointments with me. She drove me to countless appointments, to watch the doctors do basically nothing. She would shake her head in amazement because all they seemed to do was touch my pulse; touch my wrist, neck, and ankle; chat a bit; and send me home. It seemed like different doctors were asking to see me weekly to do the same thing. I saw my primary care physician, rheumatologist, pulmonologist, cardiologist, neurologist, and a host of technicians.

Toya stood by helplessly, watching me try to blow unsuccessfully during pulmonary function tests. She would call for her husband's assistance as she whisked me off to emergency rooms and numerous doctor's visits. I remember her husband having to lift me out of my car into her car because I was immobilized with chest pains. He would take my son back to their house, where he and their children made sure he was safe and not alone trying to shoulder my illness. They always took great care of him. Her family was so kind to us. Toya called me at home daily, all hours of the day and night to check on me.

Much kudos to the people from that small family church! They supported me in every possible way. Different ones came at all times and made sure my son and I had cooked food and groceries available. The pastors and the congregants alike visited us, prayed, called, and sent cards, money, whatever they could do to show us we really did matter to them. They were all phenomenal. We came to understand that we were family, and they sincerely cared and loved us.

Even the young people got in on it. A young man named Daniel came by every day after work to wash my dishes, take out the trash, and drive me wherever I needed to go. He was such a blessing. The blessing in that was I really didn't even know him like that. All he knew was where I lived and there was a need at my house. The young people would come over to my house just to hang out and spend time with us.

A shout-out to the employees of my place of employment; they too got in on what God was doing in our lives. Donated leave came in abundance. Some took my son to his sports practices and attended his games when I couldn't. He stayed at their homes to make sure he didn't miss school. One of the units paid for a housekeeping service to come and clean my apartment. Coworkers were taking me to the doctor and visiting me in and out of the hospital. They called me relentlessly.

What am I saying in this? I am saying God's grace and mercy was really working in my situation. God uses whomever is willing and available to be used by him. I have learned it is not who you think should come through for you that God uses, it is whom God has purposed for that moment, and He uses them how He sees fit. He really does know what we need and when we need it. He really is "an on-time God."

God uses people to bless us in many unexpected ways, and people do what they are able to do. In the scheme of things, every way someone chose to demonstrate their love and concern to my son and me was much appreciated. Their kindness showed the depth of God's love for us. No area of our lives went untouched or unnoticed; from that day to this, we are still and will always be eternally grateful.

# Decisions, Decisions

The clock was ticking, and I was not getting any better. I had to get up and fight. I couldn't continue to be home from work, sleeping and making meaningless visits to the doctor. The doctors overseeing my care at the time were clearly at a loss. The many pointless visits and lack of discussions regarding my treatment indicated they really understood the magnitude of the disease but it was beyond their scope of expertise. How does a doctor tell his/her patient they really don't know how to treat them? The question that loomed was serious: were they allowing their ego or reputation to drive the bus? I wonder because they were not treating me, and they were not telling me they were clueless about the best course of action.

  Things were seemingly going downhill rapidly. At some part of this journey, I remember asking my brother and sister-in-law to care for my then eight-year-old in the event I didn't make it. They agreed to my request but, not understanding the complexity and seriousness of this mystery illness, they were bewildered by my request. They didn't understand, and I couldn't explain it, because the doctors were not telling me much because of their own lack of knowledge. Also, it seemed like my only complaint was I was continuously very sleepy and the doctors were not allowing me to return to work.

I highlight this moment only as a way to bring to light the magnitude of my condition and the weight of decisions I had to shoulder alone, balancing single parenting as I navigated this very difficult time in my life. This again was a very lonely time for me.

I was supposed to meet with my attorney, who was my son's godmother, and have her draw up a will. My main concern at the time was to make sure my son was not taken away from the only family he knew if I didn't make it.

I recall my last visit to my rheumatologist. I was asleep in his waiting room for the absolute last time. Remember the doctor who flippantly told me if this or that didn't work then it was a heart and lung transplant that was needed? When I finally awoke from my routine of sleeping in his waiting room (or wherever I went), his receptionist—a husband-and-wife team—secretly had a word with me.

They said, "We have been watching you come here, and we have to tell you, he is not treating you. We can't stand by silently any longer. He really doesn't know how to treat you. Here are your charts. Go find a doctor that knows what to do for you. We don't want to see you die."

Also, the man whom I was involved with at the time was really awesome to me in many ways. He was the kind of man you definitely would want to bring home to Mama. The only problem with him was he was not called to my fight. Although he cared about me and I really could count on him for many other things, this fight for my life was not his calling. I now understand he was not called to the purpose and plan God has for my life. Some relationships are designed to last for only a season, so stop trying to give them a lifetime call.

I understand the plan and call God has for our respective lives are different, but yes, at the time without understanding, I was hurt the man whom I was dating couldn't fully commit to the battle. When I told him what the doctor and the receptionists shared with me and of my decision to take matters into my own hands by getting a second opinion and seeking a qualified doctor, his response was startling: "Why do you need to get a second opinion? Why can't you just accept what the doctor said? He is the expert, and knows what he is talking about."

Hurt, I looked at him and said, "Because it is my life, and I have an eight-year-old to live for. If it was your life that hung in the balance, you probably would be seeing things much differently."

Rejection and hurt immediately turned to anger mixed with determination. How could the man I was crazy about suggest I just lay down and die? Feeling rejected and dejected, I made up in my mind I was valuable and I would fight for my own life.

# Turning of the Tides

Toya learned of a lady named Angela who was diagnosed with lupus for many years. I never met her face-to-face, but she was a tremendous support to me over the telephone. She shared with me how lupus had affected her kidneys and her life. She was undergoing chemotherapy. She taught me all about advocating for myself and how to be tuned into my body.

It is important to listen to your body. Be kind to it. Lie down when it tells you it is tired. Plan ahead. If you are going to have a big or busy event, plan to take off the day before or the day after. Protect your health. Say no when you can't do it. Don't allow others to guilt you into overworking. Stay away from stress.

She helped me understand having lupus and pulmonary hypertension was not an automatic death sentence. My telephone mentor told me what to look for in a doctor, what questions to ask and, most importantly, told me not to be afraid to ask questions. She taught me I had to become my own best advocate.

After speaking with Angela, I suddenly awoke from my sleep long enough to make some necessary phone calls. I have since learned Angela passed away on January 2, 2013.

I called over to Georgetown Hospital and explained to the receptionist I had been diagnosed with lupus, and was also recently diagnosed with pulmonary hypertension and I needed to be seen by a doctor who understood it. She made the appointment for me to be seen by one of her doctors but, in the same breath, said, "Why don't you go to a PH [pulmonary hypertension] clinic?"

I was shocked when she said that, because for months I had been going to doctors and not one doctor had mentioned to me there was such a thing as a PH clinic.

"Where are these clinics located?" I asked.

She told me there was one at Johns Hopkins Hospital, Fairfax Hospital, and in Philadelphia. I couldn't believe what I was hearing. I was becoming cautiously hopeful.

The next step, I called my insurance company and got a listing of doctors who accepted my insurance. I was off to interview new doctors. I planned to get rid of the team of doctors that were managing my care. I was going to take control of this giant called pulmonary hypertension. I was no longer going to be pushed around.

I also called John Hopkins Hospital and spoke to someone who asked me to fax them my chart. I had everything they needed. I had an appointment all set and ready to go. I felt even more hopeful that I was on the right track now. I then called Fairfax Hospital, and much to my surprise, I got the medical director Dr. Steve Nathan, of the Heart and Lung Transplant Clinic on the line. I introduced myself, and he said, "Rosalind Frazer, I know your name."

Puzzled, I asked, "How could that be? We have never met."

He said, "Your name came up in a meeting."

I wanted to know what they were talking about and why no one ever called me. He set up an appointment to meet with him within two or three days.

In a few days, I came to the appointment to meet with him. Not only was Dr. Nathan present but also there was a team of other doctors and residents at the visit. They wanted to see this once-healthy young dancer—with a relatively unspectacular medical history, now diagnosed with PH, a rare disease—walk a short distance in the hall. It felt as though they were asking me to walk an entire football field. I was so exhausted and out of breath I could barely stand. I just wanted to sit down and go to sleep.

They all hovered around me as Dr. Nathan delivered some more seemingly devastating news. "You definitely have PH, it is progressing aggressively. On a scale of 1 to 10, 10 needing a lung transplant, you are about a 9 unless we quickly get you on an infusion pump that you will stay connected to twenty-four hours a day, 365 days a year for the rest of your life."

I couldn't accept that. I told them I thought they were wrong. I suggested I was probably having difficulty walking because I was very sleepy and I needed to rest. I told them I was sure after I went home and slept, I would return in a few days, walk the distance again, and do better.

They agreed to allow me to try again, which I now know they understood I needed to be convinced the pump really was the only necessary way to go.

I returned in a few days, and nothing had changed. I thought I was going to go home, sleep, and then get up and walk stronger and longer. Instead, I simply went home and went to sleep—no energy. When I returned to the clinic, I had already prayed and spoken to my pastor. I made a decision I would go ahead and get the pump. At this point, all I was looking for was a change in the trajectory I was on.

# A Gift

Her name was Cynthia; she was the nurse coordinator assigned to my case. Cynthia was without a doubt sent by God. I didn't know it until I sat down with her. I don't remember what prompted the conversation about my faith, but immediately, she began to encourage me about God's love for me. She began to quote the Word of God and encouraged me to fight. She told me I was not going to die but live to declare the works of the Lord. She told me I had to believe God and I had to fight. As far as she was concerned, I was assigned to her by God. I had to believe her and trust what she was saying because I couldn't see what she was telling me for myself.

She told me about other women living on the pump, and she arranged for me to meet them, if I was interested. One I could meet in person and others I could speak with on the telephone. I couldn't imagine this pump Cynthia and the doctors were talking about. All I could envision was this monstrous dinosaur machine that I would be connected to as I lay in bed twenty-four hours a day.

She told me my idea was wrong, it would be connected to my chest and I would take it wherever I went. I still couldn't envision what she was talking about, but she remained confident it was going to work. She also connected me with a specialty pharmacy that was going to help me navigate this entire medical process.

Cynthia arranged for me to speak to a few women on the phone, as promised. In between my routine of sleeping, transporting my son to and from school, and sleeping in the car at his baseball games, I was able to connect with these women and receive words of encouragement. They assured me my life would radically change from where I currently was.

I explained my fatigue and symptoms. They were certain my life quality would improve radically as soon as I got on the pump. It was hard to believe, everything was so tiring for me. I could barely stay awake. It took me at least two hours to take a shower. I felt as though I had done a hard day's work at a construction work site, from the time I started my shower, finished, and got back in the bed. To turn over in bed felt like there was an elephant lying next to me that I was pushing and it refused to be nudged.

Walking whenever I had to do it was exhausting. Climbing a flight of stairs took me getting mentally prepared at the bottom of the stairs. I would stand at the bottom and look to the top; it would take me at least fifteen to twenty minutes to get from the bottom to the top. I literally felt as though I was going to pass out when I got to the top until I sat down. These women couldn't possibly have experienced what I was experiencing. It was hard to believe the pump would lessen these symptoms.

# Angels

There was a time in my life when I thought it was reasonable to expect your family members and the people you count as close friends to be the ones who will be there for you in your time of need, because they're blood and you're close. What I have learned, God uses whom he wants to use.

During my time of illness, God used people I hardly knew to support me in all kinds of ways I would have thought only a select few close friends and family members were capable of doing. My friend, hear me. The reality is, be open to allow God to use whom he chooses. He definitely sends the right person, with the right temperament, heart, perseverance, and willingness at the right time. I have learned not to hold expectations over people's head and receive whom God sends, because they will fulfill that role in a way that will build your faith and trust in God's love for you until the day you leave this earth.

I was scheduled to have the surgery to be connected to an infusion pump (a medical device) in a few days. Kelly, one of the women who volunteered to reach out to me via telephone when asked by the doctor's office, promised to come by so I could see the pump as she wore it and lived her life on it. She came as promised, and I couldn't believe it, she looked normal. She was a tall, slim young woman. She had two young adult sons and a grandbaby, and a fanny pack around her waist.

The pump, I was told, would become my lifesaver. She took it out of her fanny pack and showed me everything about how it worked and how it was connected in her chest. She was 100 percent transparent. I was lying on the floor the entire time she visited. I could barely get off the floor. As I lay on the floor, all I could do was hope and pray the results for me would really turn out the way she said it would. She kept telling me she too used to lie on the floor and she really understood how I was feeling. I was enjoying her visit, but she really understood the fatigue, so she didn't stay very long. She promised to come and visit me at the hospital the following week. I just had to get back to sleep.

The following week, she met me at the hospital as promised. The surgery went well, and of course, I was up walking shortly after the surgery. As I was doing my daily walk through the hall, I saw a friend of mine on the same floor, visiting someone else. He came to my room to say hello. I would have liked for him to visit longer, but in about fifteen minutes, Kelly informed him I needed my rest and he had to leave. She really took her assignment seriously. LOL. She had been where I was now venturing. Surprisingly, to me—but not to the medical staff—I was getting stronger daily. I couldn't believe the fatigue was lifting, and I could once again really walk faster than a step at a time without the incredible fatigue.

While in the hospital for at least a week after the surgery, the medical team understood the seriousness of my illness, and the use of the pump was new to them. Only certain nurses were trained on how to operate the pump. Anytime the pump sounded an alarm—meaning the tubing was obstructed, preventing the medication from getting into my pulmonary artery—the nurses would respond quickly. This only created added anxiety for me. I couldn't see how I was going to go home and be safe. I also needed someone to come and learn how to mix the medication before I could be approved to go home.

One of my coworkers, Cynthia, offered to come and stay at my house for a week. She was a young woman who was going through a very painful separation. She stayed at my house for a week and helped with the wound care, cooking, and care of my son. She drove me wherever I needed to go, which was a huge blessing. The thought of going home to an apartment alone with my eight-year-old and this pump was too much for me to handle.

Another coworker came and learned how to mix the medication. Without this, my discharge would not have been approved if someone didn't come forward to learn how to mix. You are probably wondering where my family members were at this time. It really was not feasible for them to learn how to mix the medication, because the person needed to be close enough to get to me and do the mixing whenever I wasn't feeling well. My family and I were living in neighboring states, so in the event they were needed, they really were too far away to be of assistance. Tsehay, who lived closer to me, agreed to learn to mix the medication, in case she was ever needed, and thanks be to God, I never needed her assistance.

Some additional friendships were birthed in this journey as well. I would be remiss if I didn't mention two of my best girlfriends, Cheryl and Marilyn.

My friend Cheryl and little Miss Novie

Cheryl and I became friends back in the early 1990's before my son was ever a thought in my mind, we met on the job, she was a full time temporary employee with the county. I was saved when I met Cheryl and she was one of those persons who would let you know, she was "saved" in her own way. She was living life on her own terms and that was fine with her. I would boldly share my faith, she would listen and voice her doubts about Christians and that was as far as I could see in the way of impact This didn't stop our relationship from growing, we enjoyed the talks. Cheryl was a smoker at that time and I remember her, at least one time spending the night with Ingrid and me to attend church with us.

Eventually, she became a permanent employee so her job description and location changed and we no longer had much contact. I remember running into her briefly after my job site changed and she excitedly told me the wonderful news, she had gotten saved and was no longer smoking, I was so happy for her and grateful to God!

A few more years went by and additional changes occurred and we ended up working in the same unit again. By this I was struggling with health issues, but we were able to share about our faith and the goodness of Jesus!

She was eventually sent to a different job outside of the department because of a R.I.F. situation, but we remained in contact. Cheryl and I slowly became close friends and to this day she has been such a support to me, during my illness and otherwise. She is literally a part of my family. She and I did a lot together, including attending my family functions. My siblings and mother would always ask for her and wanted to know where she was and how she was doing, if we weren't together.

Who would have thought? I thank God for my friend and for the bond he created between us.

Me and Ms. Marilyn

Then, there is my sweet friend Ms. Marilyn, as I affectionately call her. I met Ms. Marilyn at a church, "The Father's House" in 2004. I found this church on the internet. I was really really in a broken place when I found this church. At that time, I was dealing with some serious hurt from two break ups. I was in the throws of a church hurt situation, a bad relationship break and my health was in crisis.

When I started attending prayer meetings at this small church, I had made one of those inner vows, I would never get close to church folk again.

I recognized Ms. Marilyn from my office. She worked in a different program in the same office and I wasn't happy about seeing her. I didn't know her and I certainly didn't want my personal business intertwined in any with my job. I was very sick physically and emotionally.

One day after prayer meeting Ms. Marilyn came up to me and offered her number on a piece of paper and said, " I don't know why, but the Lord told me to give you my number." I reluctantly took the paper, stared coldly and said " Thanks." All the while thinking to myself, " I don't know why, cause I 'm never gonna call you."

A few weeks passed maybe a month or two and I hadn't called Ms. Marilyn. By now I was still not released to return to work so I was home alone with Kelly, our family dog. I had enrolled my son in military school and he was unhappy. Regarding my health, things were really getting worse.

One day I decided to check my email and there was an email from Marilyn with no message. I thought about ignoring it but I thought it would be rude if she was waiting for a response from me. I decided to call her and let her know I didn't receive her message. It turned out to my embarrassment, she wasn't even trying to contact me, her email had gone out to all of her contacts in error. Well that my friend had to be the Lord, we began to talk and as I was sharing some crazy dream with her, she could tell I wasn't doing well. She kindly asked, "Would you like me to come over?" "Yes!" was my answer. Her next question was "Do you need anything from the grocery store?" Sure enough I gave her a list.

That Sweet lady came to my house shortly thereafter with groceries and until I returned to work part-time, which was months later, she would come to my house every day after work, sit and talk to me about everything, over the meals I started preparing for us, when I was able. I was fascinated with her candor about her faith journey, her parent's faith and her life. I never saw this friendship in the making. She would take me to doctor visits, emergency rooms, the grocery store and wherever else I needed to go, she was Johnny on the spot."

To this day, we are the best of friends, and I am so grateful for her wonderful husband David, who never prevented her from being there for me.

And you are probably wondering about that prayer group at "The Father's House" where I met Marilyn. We still attend that group today. Those people prayed me through to physical and emotional health. Yes, even difficult times with my son. We have prayed diligently for someone who were there just for that Tuesday night, there for a season or someone simply asking for prayer for a family member, friend, neighbor or co-worker. This group is committed to prayer and has a firm belief that, "Nothing is too hard for God." I have heard so many seemingly difficult prayers answered, along with people candidly sharing heartaches, worries, concerns, prayer requests and testimonies of the power of God and how he answered our prayers. People come and go, but the one thing I can say about the core group who consistently attends, I have never heard gossip or whispers of anyone saying, " Can you believe, so and so?"

    I share about these angels and friends because it is through these people God brought me to a place where I can forgive, trust and believe in people again. I know he uses and works through whom he chooses. I trust him with his choices.

# The Process

My journey was by no means over; instead, it was really just beginning. Many hospital admissions, countless doctor visits to follow, and months of being home from work, church, and many other activities. As I attempt to chronicle this part of my journey, it is a challenge to remember the road traveled without difficulty. The road traveled was belabored with unpredictability, chunks of missing spans of time because of the many kinds of powerful medications I was on. I was in and out of hospitals for different lengths of times, countless emergency room visits, the lupus in its active state creating other medical complications, etc.

About seven months after the surgery, I finally returned to work on a limited schedule and I could attend church again. At the time, the program manager at my job made a decision concerning reassigning my position and my job duties. At first, I was not enthused about being transferred from the field to a "desk job." I really enjoyed being an investigator and the day-to-day unpredictable challenges of working with clients. I worried that my new role of doing social work over the phone as opposed to in the field face-to-face with clients would be unfulfilling and boring. Thirteen years later of being out of the field, I can truly say this was the hand of God again working all things together for my good (Rom. 8:28).

Me and my supervisor, Jim

My new supervisor, Jim, was really a godsend. He was and always has been very kind to my son and me. He was very sensitive to my illness and needs. I was in and out of the hospital under his watch for several years. It felt like this journey of being unstable in my health was never going to end.

The most amazing thing to me is having a boss as consistent as Jim for the past thirteen years. Whenever I became suddenly ill and had to be rushed to the hospital or be out of work for extended periods of time, he never hesitated to rearrange his schedule to accompany me to the emergency room or check in regularly to see how I was doing.

Every time 911 was called to the office, he was always by my side until a family member was contacted and present. My son was never forgotten during these times of emergencies. Jim really was sent by God. I always refer to him as the best boss, because to me, he really has been.

He has even gone so far as attending most of my son's football games simply to show his support for us. He has done whatever he could to help out with the handyman jobs I've needed around my house. I must add, this is not something he does only for me; this is just the kind of person he is to everyone he interacts with. He really is a kind soul.

Not to create controversy, but this is one retired police officer I must say is really a very nice and compassionate person. I have never heard a person speak a bad word about Jim. Under his leadership, I was able to really focus on my health and getting better.

I was able to return to a community college and retake at least eighteen hours of lost credit hours toward my undergraduate degree. After much confusion and frustration, I officially obtained my bachelor of science degree in health and human professions in August 2004. Immediately following, I applied to Virginia Commonwealth University to the master of social work program, where I graduated in May 2009.

The road to recovery has been long and arduous, but my boss and my colleagues have been a tremendous support as they supported me and made my physical healing and recovery a success.

# A Longing

As I was going through this very difficult time in my life, the hand of God was very visible to me. I wish I could say from that point to this my son and I lived happily ever after. However, as we all keep living, life keeps happening. It was not a question anymore for me if God was able to take care of us, even in the midst of trouble; He had shown he was more than able, because he has hands and feet in the earth.

The issue for me was really about resolving the spirit of rejection, abandonment, and loneliness. The longing for a spouse seemed to drive so many of my bad impulsive decisions. Unless you have the gift of singleness, the desire for a good spouse is a sincere desire.

I was listening to a radio program the other day, and they were talking about the husband having and being given such an incredible opportunity to move toward his wife as he ministers to her soul, and the wife moving toward her husband and receiving from him the safety he gives her as he bears up under challenges instead of being crushed by them. I thought that was powerful, as the speaker drew his analogy from the movements of sexual intimacy in the marriage bed. I believe a high percentage of women who desire marriage really find security, confidence, and great worth in being in healthy marriages and in nurturing others.

The desire for marriage was and still is very alive inside of me. I believe now it is more controlled because of an impulsive decision I made back in 2003 that could have… devastated me . . . But God! But God, in his grace and mercy, stepped in and said, "No! You can't and won't destroy her."

I met a young widower after I had come to my new life on the pump. We seemed to desire the same things in life as we attempted to navigate the places we had found ourselves. The only difference as far as I could see, which I thought we could navigate, was the fact he was Muslim and I was Christian. I really thought and hoped we could navigate our way around this "eyebrow raiser." Maybe, just maybe I was wrong on my interpretation of the Scripture, which says, "Be not unequally yoked."

> "Do not be unequally yoked with unbelievers. For what partnership has righteousness with lawlessness? Or what fellowship has light with darkness? What accord has Christ with Belial? Or what portion does a believer share with an unbeliever? What agreement has the temple of God with idols? For we are the temple of the living God." (2 Cor. 6:14)

I thought maybe with maturity and progressive thinking there really could be fellowship between light and darkness, Christ with Belial. However, I am here to tell you, once again God was right and I was wrong.

This man was educated, had shown himself to have very good work ethics, and most importantly, we seemed to share similar views on what really mattered in life. We decided to get married three months after we met. I knew others were not happy about my decision, but I made up in my mind I would not be dissuaded by their opinions—or anyone else's opinions, for that matter. I knew what I wanted and "needed," as far as I was concerned. I was the one who felt the longing that, at times, was crushing inside of me. I was the one haunted by my son's deep desire for a father in his life. The church

I attended was small, and mostly everyone was married excep[t a] small pocket of adults and the young people. I, for sure, was rea[dy to] take control of my destiny.

We were married in April 2003 unbeknownst to anyone. T[he] first night we were to live as husband and wife in our new house, we had an ugly argument. It turned out this was the beginning of many disagreements that led to irreconcilable differences.

I think what was most challenging for me was my health, which was rapidly declining. I remember my ex-husband telling me when I was hospitalized he thought I was faking. My health, which was once on an upward swing, was now on a downward spiral. I restarted the cycle of hospital admissions. Migraines were now an addition to my already complex medical history. My blood pressure was very high and difficult to bring under control. Added to the smorgasbord of medical complications were Sjogren's syndrome (affecting my eyes) and Raynaud's phenomenon.

Sjogren's syndrome is an autoimmune disorder in which the glands that produce tears and saliva are destroyed. This causes dry mouth and eyes, which are the most common symptoms of this syndrome. The condition may affect other parts of the body, including the kidneys and lungs. The cause of Sjogren's is unknown. In secondary Sjogren's, it occurs along with another autoimmune disorder, such as polymyositis, rheumatoid arthritis, and scleroderma, or SLE. Dry-eyes symptoms are itching eyes or feeling that something is in the eye (information taken from the ADAM Medical Encyclopedia (last reviewed on April 20, 2013). For me, it is very difficult to produce tears, and there is a slight burning sensation because of the lack of moisture.

Raynaud's phenomenon is a condition in which cold temperature or strong emotions cause blood vessel spasms. This blocks blood flow to the fingers, toes, ears, and nose. When my Raynaud's is active, I find myself freezing while others may just be cold and can easily warm themselves up. My fingers, feet, and ears would literally turn blue, as if I was frostbitten.

The secondary form of Raynaud's starts after ages thirty-five to forty, common in people with connective tissue diseases such as scleroderma, Sjogren's syndrome, and lupus. (Information taken from "What Is Raynaud's Phenomenon? Fast Facts: An Easy to Read Series of Publication for the Public," publication date April 2009).

Here I was, about four or five months into this marriage, and once again, the medical crises were severely underway due to stress, a known nemesis to lupus. As far as I was concerned, getting out of this marriage was the only way I could see to save my life. I knew God hated divorce, but I wasn't convinced he wanted me to stay in a verbally and emotionally abusive marriage that seemed to be leading me to a premature death before I was able to fulfill the purpose for which he created me in the earth.

To make matters worse, I became pregnant with his child, and my doctors were definitely unwavering with their position: if this pregnancy was not terminated, it would take my life. My doctor was certain just the increased blood volume during my pregnancy would end my life. Not feeling very optimistic about my health, I followed the doctor's recommendation and terminated the pregnancy. Neither my faith nor my health was up to challenge his medical opinion.

Once again, I was faced with the decision of whether or not I was really pro-life or pro-choice. If I had thought the decision of being pro-life versus pro-choice was easy and that I would never come to test my faith again, I was clearly mistaken. Here I was a second time standing before God and having to make a decision.

Once again, I didn't dream in my younger days when I was conveniently pro-choice I would be faced with making these difficult decisions. Now, this time, it was my life or my unborn child's life. I do believe God's grace is sufficient for the difficult predicaments we find ourselves in, so we made a decision for me to live because my eight-year-old son needed his mother. After the procedure, I agreed to the recommended tubal ligation.

While at the hospital, having my tubal ligation, there was a parade of doctors and residents who entered my room, with the doctor telling his students he wanted them to see a patient who had numerous medical issues. I will never forget them looking at me as though I was an anomaly.

Then one doctor shook his head and piped u[p]... major-league illnesses." They couldn't believe I was fu[nctioning as] well as I was with such a smorgasbord of illnesses.

The support I thought being married would afford [was] nonexistent. The companionship I thought I would have was [also] very elusive. My husband, in his own hurt and dissatisfaction, was unsympathetic to my feelings. With my health issues and other unresolved emotional issues that consumed me, I was unable to see his pain. Instead of us making a decision to die to ourselves, we bailed on each other. We found ourselves in the predicament many couples find themselves in because they refuse to consider each other's needs. Sometimes it takes dying to self and allowing your own pain to take the backseat so another could live.

Unfortunately, neither one of us were willing to die so the other might live. We went to counseling once, and it was there I realized I was not interested in reconciliation. Living with him after that was increasingly miserable, and all I wanted to do was escape the emotional pain and physical sickness that had again become my story.

Five months later, I moved out of the house and purchased a condo. What a relief it was to be in my own place with my son. It felt like a heavy yoke was lifted off me, and when the divorce was finalized six months later, I had learned a valuable lesson: the void in you can only be filled by Christ. Trying to replace that empty space with anything other than Christ will quench your thirst only for a little while. We really must trust God to fill our empty spaces before we sit down at the table with an insatiable appetite.

# Resilience

Resilience: (1) the ability of a substance or object to spring back into shape; elasticity; (2) the capacity to recover quickly from difficulties; toughness.

    As time went on, it was my son and me at it again. This time, I had a greater appreciation and contentment with my singleness. Being married had taught me a great lesson. Whatever state you find yourself in, be content and allow God to heal your brokenness and fill the empty space inside of you. Many times we bypass God and self-medicate with unhealthy habits that temporarily fill the void or soothe the pain (i.e., using sex, substances, shopping, partying, relationships, and many other acts of escapism). I learned these methods are only temporary, and more times than not, they leave us more sad, depressed, and angry, and for some of us, we are left feeling ashamed, guilty, or condemned.

> "I am not saying this because I am in need, for I have learned to be content with whatever I have. I know what it is to be in need, and I know what it is to have plenty. I have

*learned the secret of being content in any and every situation, whether well fed or hungry, whether living in plenty or in want." (Phil 4:11, 12)*

My advice to you, don't try to fill the empty spaces with temporary things that only make you feel better for a short time. Go to God, ask him to show you the root cause of your pain, and allow him to bring permanent healing into your life. You will be surprised to discover what you are longing for is deep healing and redemption.

Like Jesus told the Samaritan woman at the well:

*"But whoever drinks the water I give them will never thirst. Indeed, the water I give them will become in them a spring of water welling up to eternal life." (John 4:13)*

I urge you to come and let him tell you who you are. Don't run away from him. Run *to* him he really is able to bring healing to your brokenness. In the words of Dr. Stevenson, "Let God explain your past, interpret your present and tell you where you are going." Do not lose heart, he will not leave you in your wounded state *"He who began a good work in you will be faithful to complete until the day of Jesus Christ" (Phil. 1:6).*

When he heals you, never again will you be like a dog returning to his vomit. *Matthew 5:6 says, "Blessed are those who hunger and thirst after righteousness, for they will be filled."*

This time, I found contentment in my singleness. As time went on, I applied to graduate school and was accepted. This was an arduous and grueling time for me. Single parenting, managing my health, and going to school all at the same time was a lot. However, because I was certain God had opened this door for me at this time of my life, I was determined to see it through to the end.

My employer was paying for their employees to return to school and obtain a graduate degree, if desired. Although this was not the perfect time, I knew it was the appointed time. Because I believed in my heart without a shadow of doubt this was the Lord's will for me, I went to school for four years part time, was in and out the hospital, was fulfilling my parental responsibilities to my son and the require-

aduate school. I couldn't even entertain the thought of [a] semester until my health had fully stabilized.

[An]d if God presents you with an opportunity and you [kn]ow it is from God, forge forward. Don't wait for everything to be perfect before you start the course. In my experience, things are never perfect and will never be perfect. I see people putting off tomorrow for what they can start today. Start and keep going. Things will be tweaked and fine-tuned as you go. Half the battle is starting. Your strength will come through your determination.

I am blessed to say with a humble and grateful heart I graduated from Virginia Commonwealth University with my masters in social work in 2009. The following year, the tuition reimbursement program was terminated and the satellite campus was being dissolved. My graduating class was the last to go to graduate school with two full years paid for, no online classes or commuting to Richmond, Virginia. To this day, without a doubt, I can say I know I was in the total and complete will of the Father and it was a fulfilling experience to the end.

To my undergraduate professor who thought he knew the will of God for me by telling me I would never make it in graduate school because I was not "graduate school material," I am here to say only God knows the plans he has for each and every one of us.

Resilience comes through determination that we will not allow life's challenges to overtake us and o' the joy we feel when we bounce back from the thing that was intended to eliminate us from the race.

# Lo-debar

Many years later, I allowed myself to be partially involved with someone whom I thought was ready for a relationship. I should have known this person was clearly not ready because his understanding or his thoughts of what his role should be as a man in a relationship didn't align with the standard God require of a "man." Consequently, me being a woman of God and following the teachings of Christ, I knew we had mismatched thoughts, points of view, understanding, etc. Hence, we were unequally yoked. Unequally yoking oneself with someone who has a different spirit, thoughts, and ways to execute to accomplish a mission is not profitable for a successful relationship.

Numbers 13-14:8, 9 Aaron and Moses sent out spies to explore Canaan, all of the spies except two came back with a fear filled report. Joshua and Caleb held a different report. "If the Lord is pleased with us he will bring us into this land and give it to us. This is a land flowing with milk and honey! Don't rebel against the Lord, and don't be afraid of the people of the land. We will devour them like bread. They have no protection, and the Lord is with us. So don't be afraid of them." Verse 24 said Caleb had a different spirit. The other spies had a spirit that was not of God so without the same God spirit they couldn't come into an agreement to effectuate a plan to defeat the enemy.

I am not saying we can't have different ideas to accomplish a task, but the foundation of how we execute to build should reflect the thoughts and mind of God. Effectively yoking yourself with someone speaks of teamwork and coordination. If we are not both yoked together in Christ's spirit first and committed to seeking the mind of God second, it is going to be hard to accomplish much as a successful team.

The funny thing is I was aware of the check in my spirit the entire time we tried to make a connection. I knew this connection was not God's will for my life, but once again, my flesh was at war with my spirit, and I wanted my flesh to win. So I deceived myself into thinking I could win him over while in a relationship.

Although I wanted this friendship to materialize into something meaningful because of the many years of attraction we had for each other, we couldn't move past "go" because of unresolved issues in both of our lives. Not because he wasn't a nice person or I was too broken, but because we found ourselves living in a place that is so familiar to many of us. It is a place called Lo-debar.

My friend, Pastor Jenise preached a powerful message on a place called Lo-debar, a city in the Bible that I had never even given a second thought. This sermon gave me valuable insight into our situation. Out of this relationship, I came to see that we were unknowingly and unfortunately living our lives in Lo-debar. Many of us end up in Lo-debar maybe through no fault of our own, or because of choices we had made or choices others had made for us. Nevertheless, here is where we find ourselves, and here is where we will live an unfulfilled life if we never allow the Lord to deal with our sins and set us free.

What and where is Lo-debar, you may be asking. Lo-debar can be found in 2 Samuel 9:1–7. Mephibosheth, Jonathan's crippled son and King Saul's grandson, ended up there when his caretaker dropped him as she carried him, attempting to flee with him to safety. It was emergent for her to get him to safety because in those days after the death of the reigning king, it was customary for the new regime to kill off all family members of the deceased king to prevent family members from uprising against the new king.

Mephibosheth became crippled as a result of being dropped, and he ended up in Lo-debar, the place where the "injured, abused, and forgotten people go." In other words, he was put out to pasture. The place where people hide away and live a life of invisibility or obscurity. Here, they nurse their pain, brokenness, and resentment. They harbor unforgiveness, blame, depression, anger, frustration, bitterness, rejection, grief, abandonment issues, etc. The place where hurt people go and live out their lives in isolation, vowing never to be hurt again.

Many of us are in Lo-debar and don't even know it. The symptoms of Lo-debar cannot be hidden. If you research this city, you will find that psychologically many of us live in our own Lo-debar in our minds. Lo-debar is present in so many of us. We are all very familiar with the saying "Hurt people hurt other people." Lo-debar houses hurt people, who, in turn, hurt other people.

Instead of dealing with the pain experienced from past relationships and situations, we build walls and fortresses around ourselves and vow no one will ever be allowed to scale the walls we have erected, not by going over, under, around, or through them. We decide to stand guard twenty-four hours a day and make sure no one gets to the other side.

People who have been wounded and have not been healed by the Holy Spirit to have the rotted root plucked out have similar symptomology. In my friend's case there are seemingly overreactions to minor situations. In some cases, there were an inordinate amount of time at work (can be indicative of avoiding dealing with deep feelings). Having meaningful conversations or a conversation of any depth was virtually impossible, because every word was misconstrued and became a federal case. In many cases, insensitivity to the feelings of others can rule supreme because of one's focus and self-absorption in self-protection.

Unfortunately, when we don't deal with our pain in a healthy manner, our toxic behaviors continue to manifest in all kinds of ways and sadly onto the people who are closest and most important to us.

Now the truth is we all find ourselves in Lo-debar at some point and time in our lives. I see now how not only was my friend living in Lo-debar but also I myself spent years in this city of imprisonment. How did I get to a place of imprisonment, you may ask. For me, a lot of it (not all of it) had to do with the effects of casual sex (sexual relations outside of marriage or, as the millennials call it, being "friends with benefits"). The undisclosed damage that society neglects to tell us is a part of the consequence when we decide, "My body, my choice," "If it feels good, do it," or "You never buy a car without test-driving."

We encourage our young men to "sow their oats" and tell young people to experience life. There is nothing wrong with "test-driving" to make sure there is compatibility and the need to experience life before a decision is made to settle down. All these well-intended advisements are all urgings that escort so many naïve and unsuspecting people straight down the path to Lo-debar, where they will reside in the grips of unexplained defeat and lack of fulfillment for years to come if truth and deliverance don't find them soon.

Over the years, my Lo-debar consisted of intense feelings of loneliness, rejection, sadness, depression, and feelings of being unloved and cast aside. Coming in contact with others who were just as broken only added to my deep hurt, rejection, and abandonment issues. Unbeknownst to me, over the years, I thought I had gotten past these emotions only to come face-to-face with the reality that I was a prisoner to these feelings and the impact they were having on my life. They had grown roots as huge, strong, and deep as the roots of a Sycamine tree.

Only recently did I realize there was a link between my sexual past and my brokenness. These negative emotions led me down the path of depression, anger, and the act of self-medicating. I was on a trajectory of surviving rather than living.

I must confess, as a single parent of a child conceived in an unconventional way, a life that lacked sexual integrity, I parented my child right in Lo-debar. This is a very painful admission because I am now aware of the real damage I caused to myself and my relationship with my child.

There is no need to beat yourself up if you realize you have lived in Lo-debar at one time or another or if you find yourself living in Lo-debar as you read this chapter. The key is to know God is with you and is willing to trade places with you. You can relocate from Lo-debar and come dine at his table forever. The first step in moving from Lo-debar is to acknowledge you are broken, then to give forgiveness to those who were contributors. Forgive yourself, and allow the Holy Spirit to lead you on the path of your healing, deliverance, and restoration.

> *"I will restore to you all the land that belonged to your grandfather Saul, and you will always eat at my table." (2 Sam. 9:7)*

# Cargo

I believe if a wounded person harbors negative feelings such as, anger, shame, condemnation, guilt, hurt, bitterness, resentment, unforgiveness towards him/herself, others and at times even God, they may find themselves with a victim's mentality possibly carrying unresolved issues or "cargo."

While I refer to unresolved issues as lugging cargo, Peter Scazzero, the author of "Emotionally Healthy Spiritualty" likens unresolved issues to that of an iceberg. Scazzero infers, too many Christians are like icebergs, "ten percent represents the visible changes we make that others can see, but the roots of who we are continue unaffected and unmoved." The other ninety percent Scazzero says. " remains untouched by Jesus Christ until there is a serious engagement " with what he refers to as" emotionally healthy spirituality." In other words, Mr. Scazzero too may be suggesting, unless we deal with our issues at the core we will remain emotionally and spiritually unhealthy, as we unfortunately lug around cargo.

In the book of Acts 27:18, when Paul, the other prisoners, and the prison staff found themselves in a tumultuous storm, one of their instincts was to "jettison the cargo." They realized they were carrying unnecessary baggage that was neither beneficial nor helpful to them if they were going to survive this violent storm.

We also have to realize that much of the old baggage of negative emotions we lug around from place to place, person to person, and relationship to relationship, if we don't educate ourselves about its root, the damage it is causing, getting healed from it, and tossing it overboard, it will literally kill us, mentally, spiritually, emotionally, and, in some instances, physically. Suppressing, stuffing, and pushing things out of your mind and just forgetting about it is not healing, that is carrying unnecessary cargo—a strategy too many people are accepting of, especially in the African American Christian community.

History for black women has always demanded them to "buck up" and drive on. We tell ourselves and believe we can't afford to lie down and die. While that is true, the flip side is also true, that we should afford ourselves to lie down to live. We tell ourselves we can't show weakness or stop for a minute. The truth is by not caring for ourselves we neglect ourselves, which perpetuates anger within us synonymous to another violation and hence we become what others refer to as "the angry black woman." The truth is, when bad things happen, it can take a while to work through the pain and emotions to once again feel safe and return to the sound, whole person God created us to be. With the right treatment, support, and definitely with the help of the Holy Spirit, we can have a healthy recovery.

Five Flowers

    Another road on my life's journey doesn't make me very proud to share, but my transparency and candor was and still is critical in my healing more than thirty years later. I must tell of my five flowers.
    Who would have thought when I selfishly, carelessly, and ignorantly made decisions synonymous with "my body my choice," I would look up at age fifty and proclaim that despite the pronouncement of planned parenthood, politicians, the medical community and society at large, a baby is a life from the time of conception. Today, I am unequivocally stating, life begins at conception!
    My first decision to abort my first son came at the tender age of sixteen. I saw no other way I could have a child that young and still make something of my life. So I decided that "Peniel" was only tissue and it was okay to make a decision to sacrifice his life.
    Three more times, from ages nineteen to twenty-two, I made the same decision concerning, "Hope," "Faith," and "Joy." I was in college, and they were again interruptions in the plans I had for my

life. I never once gave a second thought I was tampering with God's plan, because he doesn't make mistakes and truly children, no matter how and when they are conceived, are a gift from God. I believed the lie that I was doing the best thing for me and them and as soon as the abortion was completed it would be a huge relief and I could get back on track with my life.

Since I had never experience any nightmares or abortions-gone-awry stories, I thought there was no consequence and I had gotten away scot-free. I had it all figured out. I was at the helm of the controls, and when I did get married, my husband and I would be in love, making responsible planned-pregnancy decisions and I would never visit these decisions again. Right?

Wrong.

As a matter of fact, the final time I had to make another decision to sacrifice my fifth child, Israel, I was married and this time, the doctors gave me no choice.

The decisions I made to sacrifice these five precious flowers had an impact on my ability to bond in relationships including with my son. As I read, Ministering to Abortion's Aftermath, I learned by not acknowledging and confessing abortion as a sin and a sin of murder contributed to my feelings of stunted spiritual growth, my capriciousness and a host of other negative behaviors and emotions. Because of my confession, I finally received the courage to walk out of Lo-debar, free from self-condemnation, shame, and guilt. Now I walk in continuous joy and peace whether the storms of life are raging or calm.

I never would have guessed in a million years my attitude concerning "my body, my choice," regarding multiple relationships and abortions, would have impacted my life so drastically. In order for me to be restored, the Good Shepherd, in his wisdom and compassion, would use the very decisions that brought me brokenness to be the anecdote that would bring victory to my soul.

The following letter I wrote to God and read at the memorial service for my Five Flowers at the conclusion of my post-abortion support group:

*May 7, 2016*

*Five Flowers!*

*Dear God,*

*Today I write this short letter expressing my feelings about my five precious flowers, Peniel, Hope, Faith, Joy and Israel. Five beautiful flowers I selfishly chose not to hold in my arms, but now I hold forever in my heart. For years I tried to push them out of my mind and heart and in seven short weeks they have become more than just an unfortunate moment in my life. They are my five precious forever loves.*

*Father, if you are willing, let them know from my heart to theirs. Peniel you were my first, whenever, I call your name I realize I came face to face with God and lived. Hope, the scripture says, "if we hope for what we do not yet have, we wait for it patiently." I patiently wait to see you face to face. Faith, today I begin with fond thoughts of you and with courage I press towards the future. Joy, you bring a heart full of smiles to me and Israel, I will always remember, so young, you were the sacrificial lamb. We will forever share an eternal bond.*

*My children, we never got a chance to meet each other, but I believe if you were given a chance you would have brought a smile to not only my face, but God's face as well.*

*Finally, I can have peace as I have reconciled you all in my heart and soul. I know you are safe in our Father's arms. I love you all with the everlasting love of the Father. I will think of you all daily until we meet again.*

*Love you guys madly,*
*Mom*

# The Orphan Spirit

In an article written by David Hino, he defines the orphan spirit as a "person who lacks emotional identity and seeks to earn his identity through his/her efforts. Their symptoms, he said, include a critical spirit, being defensive, unable to take correction, feeling abandoned and blaming others."

Additionally, Joseph Mattera said, the person with an orphan spirit experiences a sense of loneliness, abandonment, alienation, isolation, and rejection. I myself am not an expert on the spirit of the orphan or any spirit for that matter, but from my research I would say, there appears to be a strong relationship between the orphan spirit, the spirit of rejection and the spirit of rebellion. According to Mattera, the orphan spirit started almost instantly after the fall of Adam and Eve. Essentially, a person with an orphan spirit feels as though they have to earn the love and acceptance of their father rather than accept it was given to them simply because they are his child. God has adopted us into his family; therefore, we are his children, heirs to his throne and entitled to all he has simply because of "grace," not because we have to work and earn anything.

In the article "The Difference between the Orphan Spirit and a Spirit of Sonship by Mattera, J." a comprehensive list between the two is listed. I chose only to list the traits of the orphan spirit.

*The traits of the orphan spirit are as follows:*
1. *Operates out of insecurity and jealousy*
2. *is jealous of the success of his brother*
3. *serves God to earn the Father's love*
4. *tries to medicate its deep internal alienation through physical stimulation*
5. *is driven by the need for success*
6. *uses people as objects to fulfill goals*
7. *repels children*
8. *has fits of rage*
9. *is always in competition with others*
10. *lacks self-esteem*
11. *receives its primary identity through material possessions, physical appearance, and activities*

I believe these traits manifest in a vast majority of people because we were all impacted by the fall of Adam and Eve, and in today's society, so many are impacted by the absent father, be it physically, emotionally, or psychologically. Looking at these negative traits and senses, many can identify with the effects of one trait or another because they didn't know to settle: "I am his and he loves me. Therefore, I can do nothing to earn his love or conversely lose his love."

If we do not effectively resolve the difference between the orphan spirit and the spirit of sonship inside of us, we may find ourselves living out the negative consequences of the orphan spirit. Consequently, we may find ourselves stagnated, hindered, and devoid of forward momentum and subsequently living beneath our potential in a dissatisfied manner.

It is imperative that we stop, process, and heal. Earnestly examine and analyze what we are sincerely feeling, the behaviors that are manifesting as a result, and what our coping strategies are. We must then seek to find healing from God through reading his Word and prayer. True healing comes when we submit to God and cooperate with his timing and the way in which he chooses to heal.

Educating ourselves with truth and about the effects our experiences have had on us is essential if we are to obtain complete healing. If we neglect to do this, we live out the effects of death in our lives through unhealthy emotions and mucho broken relationships.

Recently, I have become cognizant of the fact that people have been ignoring very critical experiences in their lives, stuffing them or merely pretending they didn't happen so there is no need to address them and find true healing. This, my friend, is a very dangerous and unproductive way to treat yourself, and it does nothing positive for you except cause you to behave like an orphan.

For many years, I thought I demonstrated strength by not acknowledging and not dealing with hurt and pain, but the results of avoidance have only caused me to make poor decisions and operate out of the deep hurt of rejection, loneliness, isolation, and abandonment more deeply than I could ever imagine. I thought I was heroically pressing on in battle.

What causes the orphan spirit? Situations that thrust us into a place where we are left to feel like the only person I can depend on is myself; hence, I feel unsafe and insecure.

Consequently, we find ourselves nursing feelings of rejection, abandonment, isolation, alienation, and loneliness. Then it becomes difficult to receive unconditional love and acceptance from the Father. I heard Dr. Matthew Stevenson and a few of his colleagues in the ministry discussing the orphan spirit. Their discussion was so enlightening to me about my own condition that I had to research it a little further for my own understanding and deliverance.

Like how a natural orphan is separated from his/her natural parents for various reasons, we in the spiritual sense have all been separated from our Heavenly Father because of sin's entrance into the world. *Ezekiel 16:1–5* said, *"On the day you were born your cord was not cut, nor were you washed with water to cleanse you, nor rubbed with salt, nor wrapped in swaddling cloths. No eye pitied you, to do any of these things to you out of compassion for you, but you were cast out on the open field, for you were abhorred, on the day that you were born."*

We all, by God's account, were abandoned and left in the fields to wallow in our own blood, unwanted. I believe this occurred after the fall of Adam and Eve. God himself came by, saw us, chose us, cleaned us up, cleansed us, and commanded us to live. He placed fine linen upon us, fed us with fine foods, adorned us with precious jewels, and made us flourish as a plant of the field.

As you can imagine, being orphaned as a newborn baby without the nurturance and love of parents/caretakers creates a plethora of psychological, emotional, and mental difficulties. Rejection and abandonment affects people in many ways. One way that hit home for me is the fact that I was raised without my father. I am the product of an adulterous relationship, so I never really got to know my father or spend intimate quality time with him. Therefore, I tried to find acceptance and love through relationships and false intimacies.

In Ezekiel 16:33, God said to Jerusalem, "Men give gifts to all prostitutes, but you gave your gifts to all your lovers, bribing them to come to you from every side with your whorings. No one solicited you to play the whore, and you gave payment, while no payment was given to you; therefore you were different."

What did this mean to me? It meant, having an orphan spirit, I had a yearning for acceptance and love and I was unwisely willing to pay for love and acceptance. The person with an orphan spirit would pursue others feverishly, casting their pearls before swines (impure, malicious, and self-righteous people). We are warned not to do this because swines will only trample our wisdom and gifts underfoot then turn around and tear us into pieces.

> *"Do not give what is holy to the dogs; nor cast your pearls before swine, lest they trample them under their feet, and turn and tear you in pieces." (Matt. 7:6)*

A person with an unchecked orphan spirit will find themselves in wrong relationships, giving everything in hopes of being accepted. However, they receive little love and acceptance

receive huge doses of rejection, loneliness, and feelings of unwantedness and unworthiness because the recipient had no real intension of remaining in the relationship and giving the love and acceptance the person with the orphan spirit desired.

# First Bind the Strongman

Mark 3:27 says, "No man can enter a strong man's house, and spoil his goods, except he will first bind the strong man; and then he will spoil his house."

It occurred to me as I was writing this chapter the strongman in my life was the orphan spirit, and attached to this spirit were the spirits of rejection, abandonment, unwantedness, low self-esteem, low self-confidence, and all the negative emotions and attitudes aforementioned.

Let me take a moment right here and digest the role I acted in for many years. Yep, it is true, I played the role of one with low self-esteem and low self-confidence, as much as I touted I didn't have an esteem and confidence issue, my actions said otherwise.

There is something about admitting those words to one's self. For a woman to be told or admit she is lacking in these two categories is synonymous to attacking a man's manhood. I believe if you have low self-esteem and low self-confidence your self-respect will be low and that will account for many poor decisions.

Just recently when I shared with a friend of mine that I no longer have to settle because of low self-esteem and low self-confidence, he responded with shock. He said "You!, I never saw that in you." It was bittersweet as I said confidently. "I don't care what I said or what I pretended to be, my actions spoke volumes of the truth of what I felt, but I thank God for true deliverance and healing."

Now that is out the way, let me proceed. Why would I say this, you may wonder. I say this because of my fatherless upbringing. My father had eleven children in total, seven by his wife and four of us from mistresses. Since I didn't grow up with my father, I never really understood the depth of the impact of his absence. My mother and my older siblings loved and cared for me. My mother could only love me as a mother could, and my siblings could only love me as siblings could.

Regardless of what single parents say, especially African American women, there is no way a mother can be a "daddy and a mommy." Children need their father. A father provides security, protection, confidence, love, and worth in his child.

I never had the protection of a father. I never experienced his validation. I never had him around to glean from him the wisdom and advice I needed as a young girl and as a young adult woman (he died when I was about twenty-three or twenty-four years old). I knew my father on the surface, but never intimately. Consequently, I had no one to protect and steer me from the wolves who came to ransack my life.

So to get saved and hear and read that God is my Heavenly Father and he will take care of me and all I had to do was trust him, I had no concept of what to do and how I was supposed to implement that mind-set to make it a reality in my life. Consequently, I lived my life uncovered and vulnerable to the many wolves that came dressed in sheep's clothing, or just boldly presented themselves as wolves because they knew I had no real protector.

Up until I received knowledge and insight and were able to acknowledge my brokenness, this strongman (orphan spirit) and his many imps had a field day in my life. Then Jesus met me at twenty-one days of prayer at my church and led me to Song of Solomon

1:6: "My mother's children were angry with me; they made me the keeper of the vineyards; but mine own vineyard have I not kept."

In other words, be careful you don't preach to others and you yourself be disqualified for the prize. At that very moment, I knew I had to sit down from everything I was doing (even the good things) and cooperate and trust him with the process of my healing. I will share a key part of my healing process, but remember this is my journey and yours doesn't have to and may not look like mine. If you remember in my dedication I mentioned my prayer partner Janice. Well Janice and I met when we were about twenty two or twenty three years old and only for a short while we ever lived in the same state. Most of our friendship we have lived in different states, but we always maintained a telephone friendship, not regular but honest. We were always able to pick up where we left off even if we hadn't spoken to each other for years.

Me and my prayer partner, Janice

Around 2014 or 2015, Janice started going through a personal crisis so we began talking more frequently. Janice is saved but her relationship with the Lord was more superficial at the start of her crisis. Every time I spoke to her she was so incredibly sad, broken and crying continually. Our conversations always ended with me praying for her. I was becoming increasingly worried and burdened for her and the Lord would always direct me during my prayer time to call and pray with her. My heart was so broken and I must be honest I was worried about her mental state.

I would ask her if I could have different ones call or suggest persons she could call to speak with for answers. We were both desperate for some relief for her. Little did I know the Lord had a different plan in mind for the both of us. Out of Janice's pain direct ministry to her and for myself arose. I began seeking the Lord diligently in the scriptures and through prayer for Janice. I called her everyday and encouraged her to hang in there. We soon began to confess our secrets, shame, past experiences and all the things we vowed to take to the grave. Lo and behold we became much needed prayer partners to each other.

It is unbelievable the healing God brought to the both of us and the areas he healed in Janice that were unrelated to her initial crisis. God is so incredible, his works really are wonderful and marvelous. I would have never guessed in a million years that when I was helping Janice, the Lord also had my healing in mind. I gained many treasures out of this new relationship with Janice, but two of the nuggets I am so grateful for is the ability to now be a true friend and hang in there with someone when the chips are down. I shared with you being able to sustain relationships was a challenge for me because of my own brokenness. Now Janice and I always give him praise for now we know God as "Our father!"

I thank God for healing!!

*"A man who has friends must himself be friendly, but there is a friend who sticks closer than a brother." (Prob 18:24)*

God then removed the blinders from my eyes and unstopped my ears so I could hear the knowledge I needed. He then was able to bind the strongman and all his imps who had plundered my house in so many ways for so many years. John 8:32, 36 says, "And you shall know the truth and the truth shall make you free . . . So if the Son sets you free, you will be free indeed."

I am free! Hallelujah!

Today, I am no longer fatherless. I have a Heavenly Father—a protector, provider, validator, and advocate. I have everything a child needs in their dad to feel safe, secure, and loved. No longer am I orphaned and on my own to be plundered and devoured. No longer do I have to pay for love and acceptance.

I see now as I look back over my life the dangers and downfall of having no father, no covering. I am grateful I have been adopted as God's child. I am an heir to the throne. I am a member of the household of faith. I am accepted. I am sealed with his precious Holy Spirit and bought with his blood. No longer am I rejected, abandoned, unwanted, and alone. I have a father!

I believe God is able to restore anyone who has been in captivity to the orphan spirit. My recitation is a combination of scriptures from Song of Solomon and Romans:

> *"God has set me as a seal upon his heart, as a signet ring upon his finger and engraved me on the palm of his hand. His love is as strong as death, many waters cannot quench it, many floods cannot drown it. What can separate me from the love of God? Neither, tribulations, persecutions, distress, famine, nakedness, danger or sword, nothing can separate me from his love. My beloved's jealousy is as fierce as the grave, therefore, I will worship no other God, for the name of the Lord is jealous and he is an all consuming fire."*

# Love Is Like a Seed

One day, I was in prayer at the side of my bed, and all of a sudden, a realization, which I couldn't believe, dropped into my spirit. I was guardedly excited because I didn't want to be disappointed. I checked in with my spirit again to see if what I was aware of was still present in my heart. It was! I realized my love for Christ like a seed was planted in my heart. This was exciting for me, because for years I felt like the love many people sang and cried about seemingly genuinely was elusive to me. I would say I love God because the Bible is replete about telling about his love for us. Also, to hear others speak of their love for Christ in church services and in conversations, among other believers, I queried with myself about why I wasn't genuinely feeling that way.

    I secretly admitted to myself that although I spoke about Christ's love, I didn't really feel like I was sincerely in love with him. It is easy for my brain to accept, we believe by faith, and I can comprehend that him giving his life demonstrated his love for me. However, for years, I didn't feel I was in love with him the way others were weeping and sharing about their love and how love would keep them from certain behaviors.

I knew I was not completely sold out with my love for Christ because although I could refrain from certain behaviors for a while, if the right temptation came along, I would abandon my decision to refrain. My decision to refrain had nothing to do with my love for Christ; it was more about if the picture was right.

I wonder if this explains why many people profess to love Christ, but when you look at their behaviors, you wonder if they earnestly know Him, especially when they readily espouse the old familiar adages of "God knows my heart" or "The Spirit is willing, but the flesh is weak." Whenever I hear this scripture recited, I know what is to follow is going to be contrary to what God desires for us.

I believe one can become diligent in their efforts to deal with the core issues that linger in their hearts. In dealing with those deep issues, they would no longer need to carry this portable crutch in their bags, ready to pull it out at whim and helplessly lean on it because the battle is already lost in their mind. Renewing your mind daily by reading the Word of God, praying, getting revelation on deeply rooted hidden things in your lives, and dealing with them will help one win the seemingly hopeless battle in their heart, mind, and soul.

Unresolved issues attract little foxes, which ruin the vine and hinder our forward progress by keeping us stagnated as we march endlessly around the mulberry bush. You are probably wondering, how can you march and remain stagnant at the same time? You can march endlessly and be stagnant because you haven't received the command to "forward march."

If you don't deal with the root of your issues and be patient and honest enough to confront your past experiences and be brave and bold enough to trust God's instructions for your healing, even when it doesn't make sense, you will find yourself year after year starting and stopping at the same point of your journey. You will be like the person who ran for miles on the treadmill and never left the place where they started. Being around prophetic people in a prophetic atmosphere has also helped to shift my thinking about who I am, and helped me to see what I was created to do, thereby opening my eyes to my beloved, and now I know, "I am my beloved and my beloved is mine."

*"I belong to my beloved, and his desire is for me." (Song of Sol. 7:10)*

Today, as I sit here writing this book, I can truly say I love him because he first loved me. Because of my love for him, I choose to make right choices that please him and bring a smile to his face. This love for him I now feel also translates to love for myself and others.

For many years, I didn't really feel love for others even when I would say "I love you." Now, since my heart has been healed through the sexual-integrity teaching, the post-abortion class, confession, and prayer, I literally feel my heart is opened to both receive and give love.

LOVE is like a seed

Jadavi-le and Novie…Luv these babies!!

I met these two precious little darlings, Jadavi-le and Novie and if I can tell you how I fell in love with these two little girls as if they were my blood grandbabies. I marvel that I feel love for them when I interact with them, and I can truly say I feel my heart open to receive their love.

For me, Christ has planted a seed of love in my heart, and the more I obey him, the more I water the seed of love to grow. The negative seeds that had been planted and taken root in my heart for so many years are finally dying and disappearing. Remember the saying "What you feed will grow, and what you starve will die." Today, I feed my spirit with his Word, I strengthen it with obedience, and I starve negative emotions by renouncing them and making a decision to no longer agree with their operation.

# At Last!

The following is my testimony of finally receiving breakthrough and healing in areas of deep hurt, pain, depression, sadness, rejection, loneliness, unwantedness, anger and, finally, sexual healing. I was broken, and this was the reason for a lot of my inability to bond in healthy relationships, also the cause of broken relationships, a sense of rejection, abandonment, loneliness, and insecurities.

A lot has happened in my life concerning sexual impurity that spans as far back as my childhood, and I have learned suppression, stuffing, pushing past experiences out of my mind, or simply saying they are under the blood is not healing. Without acknowledgment, education, and complete healing, my forward momentum and growth were always compromised.

> *"They overcame by the blood of the lamb and by the word of their testimony." (Rev. 12:11)*

For years, I experienced depression, sadness, and anger and practiced self-medicating. No matter how much I prayed, fasted, spoke in tongues, preached, danced, tithed, and did all the things that were supposed to bring soundness and wholeness into my life, I could never experience sustained joy and peace. I felt as though the joy of the Lord and the peace of God were elusive to me.

On December 14, 2015, my mom passed away. That was one of the saddest days of my life, but her passing catapulted me into my journey to start on my healing journey.

Picture of my beloved mother, Margaret, affectionately called by her children, "Mommy."

In January 2016, I attended a call to twenty-one days of prayer at my church, and also a church event, which introduced new attendees to ministry activities, designed to encourage active participation in the life of the church. I met a woman at this church event named Janine.

Me and Janine -Facilitator for the Sexual Integrity presentation

One day, as I was conversing with Janine, she began to share with me the damaging effects of having casual sex with multiple partners (friends with benefits) or whatever other name we give partners outside of marriage, which if we aren't careful can translate quickly into multiple partners. It turned out Janine does seminars in different settings on sexual integrity, purity, and/or health.

She invited me to one of her teachings, and as I heard her teach, I found her words revolutionary and life changing as she explained the effects and damages casual sex with multiple partners have on a person's brain and emotions. She explained about the brain being the largest organ involved in sexual intimacy and what happens when four particular hormones—dopamine, oxytocin, vasopressin, and cortisol—are released as sex is experienced.

As I sat under the teaching and heard about the negative emotional effects—anger, depression, self-medicating—I knew immediately the Holy Spirit was speaking to me.

I later reflected on the information and acknowledged and confessed my past experiences. I asked the Lord to forgive me, and I asked specifically for healing for the damaged parts of my brain. It became clear that through Janine, the Holy Spirit had unlocked some areas and revealed some damages that for years no preaching, teaching, or counseling could tap into. Although my experiences were indeed under the blood, the ill effects were still plaguing my life.

For the first time, I was able to understand the cause of my negative emotional roller coaster and why I was having trouble bonding and staying connected in relationships with family members, friends, coworkers, and even my son.

I immediately understood the root of my brokenness and effectuated what I had learned at a prayer-and-deliverance intensive with Pastor Stephen A. Garner. I began to pray more effectively and specifically, and would you believe for the first time in over twenty-five years I was finally experiencing breakthrough, healing, sustained joy, and peace?

As I began to think upon the past I understood the effects it had on my spirit man, I was able to effectively pray for my deliverance from spirits of lust, perversion, false comforts, fornication, adultery, and negative spirits, which had attached themselves to my personality. I was able to be free from all the spirits that had dominated my life. As I began to break spiritual powers of darkness, renounce, denounce, and command my freedom from demonic strongholds, I finally began to experience deliverance, joy, and peace!

The teachings unveiled other areas I didn't know were also problematic. Janine suggested I attend an abortion-recovery group so I could complete the healing process. I was skeptical.

Me and Marilyn H. – Facilitator for the post-abortive group

After a second suggestion was made to me about considering joining the post abortion group, I hesitantly agreed. I thought to myself " This must be the Lord speaking to me." I didn't know it, but I would soon learn a lot of the negative emotions I was feeling and experiencing were very much interrelated to my past decisions of " My body, my choice."

The truth is, I never knew there was such a thing as a post-abortive group and I couldn't imagine what awaited me on that road to recovery. I decided to join the group but I was very guarded. To my amazement in the group I found five women that held on to a dark secret. We were feeling tremendous shame, guilt and desperately wanted and needed God's forgiveness. Leading the way was a woman that had been through her own recovery and was unequivocally convinced that God would meet us where we were. Her spirit was sweet, precious and loving. The eight weeks together we shed tears, we looked at a class video of an abortive recovery group, we shared our hearts, did crafts, ate, bonded, laughed, released blame, accepted and gave forgiveness, prayed and in the end through a memorial service we gave dignity to our babies. Once again, I would have never thought such deep healing awaited me and best of all not one person dropped out. To date we are still in contact.

At twenty-one days of prayer, God spoke the Song of Solomon 1:6 (God's Word Translation) "They made me the caretaker of the vineyards. I have not even taken care of my own vineyard." In other words, Paul said, "But I discipline my body and subjugate it, lest somehow after preaching to others, I myself should become disqualified" (1 Cor. 9:27).

What did that mean for me? It meant it was time for me to lie down and let the Lord commence to working on me. It was time for me to stop pretending as though I was healed and truly get healed. It was time for me to stop existing and start living. The only way that was going to be possible was if I allowed the Holy Spirit to take the lead and allow him to operate in the broken areas in my life.

Who would have thought the reason for my capriciousness, depression, anger, and self-medicating, my inability to trust God and move forward with faith were due to experiences and decisions I had made across my life span. Some were decisions other people made for me without my consent many years ago.

Today, I am on a wonderful road to healing, deliverance, and restoration. Since February 2016, I have experienced sustained joy and peace, resolved anger, genuine love, and healthier interactions with others. My son says I don't flip out like I used to. The people on my job tell me every day how much happier and friendlier I have become and how much they are enjoying this "new me." Things that would have sent me over the edge with anger or bound me in depression and cause me to self-medicate by looking for false comforts have been unable to bring and keep me at that low place.

I thank God for the teaching I have received on sexual integrity and in the post-abortion group. The peace, joy, and love of God are no longer elusive to me. I am finally free from shame, guilt, and condemnation. Jesus Christ really is a healer!

Friends, my prayer is in reading my story, your takeaway would not be to judge the life I have lived but see that in whatever your trials, tribulations, and setbacks, if you turn it over to Him and trust that really all things will work for your good, He really will give you beauty for ashes.

I am grateful that Christ really is committed to our healing, deliverance, and restoration!

My healing journey has not ended because God will never be finished with us, until he calls us home. Currently, I am finally in counseling dealing with the effects of the rape, and other violations I have encountered in my life.

I am so grateful for the work he has done in me thus far and it is with great anticipation and expectation I wait to see what else he has in store for me.

I will keep you posted so hang tight, and keep the faith until we meet again . . . Remember . . . " He who began a good work in you, will be faithful to complete it until the day of Jesus Christ."

God is not finished with you yet my friend!

"So if the Son makes you free,
you will be free indeed." (Jo 8:36)

# Contact the Author

If you answered yes to any of the questions below you may need help starting the road to your "At Last!"

1. Has unexplainable depression and sadness continually plague you since you accepted Christ?
2. Is the love of God and the joy of the Lord seemingly elusive to you?
3. Is your past holding your future hostage?
4. Is the shame and guilt of your past ever present in your thoughts and emotions?
5. Do you want to be made whole?
6. Do you want to be free from depression, sadness and the torment of your past?
7. Are you ready to walk in the joy, freedom and love of God?
8. Are you brave enough to walk victoriously in who God has created you to be?
9. Would you like a COACH to walk alongside you to Your "At Last!"

If you answered yes to any of the questions above contact me:
atlast@phrazanation.com
or 1-888-612-6996.

# About the Author

Rosalind was born on the sunny isle of St. Thomas, US Virgin Islands, to the late Robert E. Frazer and Margaret E. Walters. She is the youngest of seven siblings and is the mother of her only child, Damani, the pride and joy of her heart.

She earned a bachelor of science degree from Syracuse University and her master of social work degree from Virginia Commonwealth University. She has been a social worker for over twenty five years.

In 1991, at age twenty-five, God called and enlisted Rosalind as a soldier in the army of the Lord. Shortly thereafter, she received her calling to the ministry of evangelism. Rosalind has started working on her master of divinity degree. She currently serves on the prayer team at her church in Manassas, Virginia, and is a volunteer at a Christian unplanned pregnancy clinic.

Recently she served as a minister at Greater Deep Tabernacle of Faith in Raleigh, North Carolina. She gave her initial sermon in May 2012 at the Temple of Healing Waters COGIC, where she served as the liturgical dance director, a member of the prayer and educational ministry, and as a leader on the daily telephone prayer line.

She has served extensively in church auxiliaries on prayer teams, as founder and director, and as lead choreographer with several dance ministries. As a member at her earlier church, she founded a drill team and a "Feed the homeless" ministry. As a dance minister, she has ministered at various engagements and internationally in Dubai, United Arab Emirates.

CPSIA information can be obtained
at www.ICGtesting.com
Printed in the USA
FFOW03n2029211217
44059757-43303FF